11+ Maths

WORKBOOK 2

Numerical Reasoning Technique

Dr Stephen C Curran
Edited by Dr Tandip Singh Mann & Anne-Marie Choong

This book belongs to

Accelerated Education Publications Ltd

Contents

4. Fractions — Pages
1. What is a Fraction? — 3
2. A Fraction as a Division — 4
3. A Whole as a Fraction — 5
4. Proper Fractions — 6-7
5. Equal Fractions — 8-10
6. Simple Fractions — 10-12
7. Complex Fractions — 12-13
8. Improper Fractions — 13-17
9. Mixed Numbers — 17-19
10. Mixed Numbers and Improper Fractions — 20-22
11. Lowest Common Denominators (LCD) — 22
12. The Four Rules of Fractions — 23
13. Adding Fractions — 23-26
14. Subtracting Fractions — 27-30
15. Two Rule Fractions (+ & −) — 30-31
16. Multiplying Fractions — 31-34
17. Dividing Fractions — 34-37
18. Two Rule Fractions (× & ÷) — 37-38
19. Four Rule Fractions (+−×÷) — 38-39
20. Fractional Parts — 40-41
21. Decimals and Fractions — 41-42
22. Fractions in Size Order — 43-45
23. Fraction Problems — 45-46
24. Fraction Boxes — 46-49
25. Fraction Number Lines — 50
26. More Fraction Problems — 51

5. Money and Costs
1. Units of Currency — 52
2. Pounds and Pence — 52
3. Money Calculations — 53
4. Money Problems — 53-55
5. Costs — 55-56
6. Currency Conversions — 56-57
7. Profit and Loss — 58
8. Unit Costs — 59
9. More Money Problems — 60

6. Measurement — Pages
1. Metric Measures — 61-62
2. Metric Conversions — 62-63
3. Metric Calculations — 64-65
4. Imperial Measures — 65
5. Metric-Imperial Conversions — 66-67
6. Estimating Measurements — 68-69
7. Reading Metric Scales — 70-71
8. Temperature — 71-74
9. Measurement Problems — 74-75

7. Averages
1. Mode, Median and Range — 76-78
2. The 'Mean' or Average — 78-80
3. More Average Problems — 81

8. Bases
1. What is a Base? — 82
2. Base 2 (Binary) — 82-84
3. Counting in Other Bases — 84-86
4. Multiplying Bases — 87-88
5. Dividing Bases — 89-90
6. Mixed Exercises — 90

Chapter Four
FRACTIONS
1. What is a Fraction?

A **Fraction** is part of a whole. It has a top and bottom half.

$\frac{1}{2}$ — 1 - **Numerator** (How many parts); 2 - **Denominator** (Total number of parts)

The line that separates the numerator and denominator is called a vinculum.

Examples: Express as fractions: a) One whole one b) One half

a) One whole

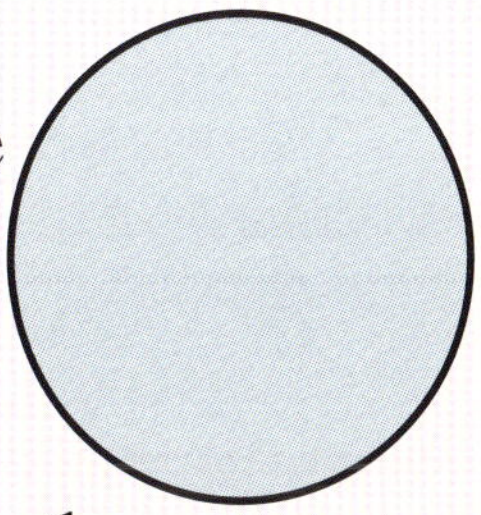

$\frac{1}{1}$ (One part) of (One part)

b) One-half

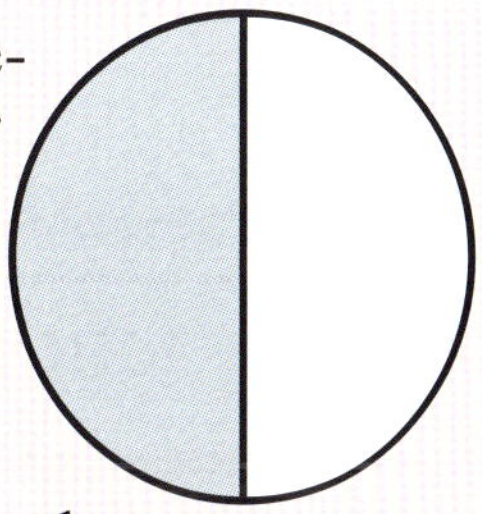

$\frac{1}{2}$ (One part) of (Two parts)

Circles are used to represent fractions. A fraction is part of any whole thing, e.g. half your pocket money. The whole one would be all of your pocket money.

Fractions are also **Multiplications**: **'of'** means 'multiply' ↓

$$\frac{1 \;\text{of}\; }{2} \quad \text{or} \quad \frac{1 \times}{2}$$

This is **half** of a whole, or $\frac{1}{2} \times 1$

Fractions are also **Divisions**: **'into'** means 'divide' ↑

$$\frac{1 \;\text{into}\; }{2} \quad \text{or} \quad \frac{1 \div}{2}$$

Fractions Comparison Chart

The larger the denominator of a fraction, the smaller its value. E.g. $\frac{1}{8}$ is smaller than $\frac{1}{5}$ because it has been split into more parts.

One whole							
Half	½						
Third	⅓	⅓					
Quarter	¼	¼	¼				
Fifth	$\frac{1}{5}$	$\frac{1}{5}$	$\frac{1}{5}$	$\frac{1}{5}$			
Sixth	$\frac{1}{6}$	$\frac{1}{6}$	$\frac{1}{6}$	$\frac{1}{6}$	$\frac{1}{6}$		
Eighth	$\frac{1}{8}$	$\frac{1}{8}$	$\frac{1}{8}$	$\frac{1}{8}$	$\frac{1}{8}$	$\frac{1}{8}$	$\frac{1}{8}$

2. A Fraction as a Division

All fractions are divisions. Therefore the line in the middle of a fraction simply means **divided by**.

Example 1: Show **2** parts divided by **3** diagrammatically.

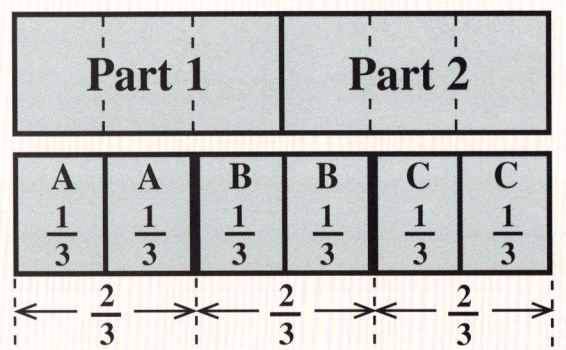

When the **two** parts are divided by **3**, each new part will be **two-thirds**.

$$2 \div 3 = \frac{2}{3}$$

Numerator - How many of each type (As, Bs, etc.)?
Denominator - How many groups of each type (As, Bs, etc.)?

Example 2:

Show **7** divided by **8** as a fraction.

7 divided by **8** written as a fraction is:

$$\frac{7}{8}$$

(**Seven** parts)
of
(**Eight** parts)

Exercise 4: 1   Write as fractions:

Numerator - Count how many of each type - As, Bs, Cs and Ds, etc.
Denominator - Count how many groupings there are in total.

1) If these **3** squares were divided into **4** equal parts, each new part could be written as the fraction ____ .

2) **4** circles were divided into **9** equal parts. Each new part is ◯ ◯ ◯ ◯ ____ .

3) **8** divided by **3**. ____

4) **9** divided by **10**. ____

5) **5** divided by **7**. ____

Write as divisions:

6) $\frac{6}{7}$ _____

7) $\frac{4}{5}$ _____

8) $\frac{2}{9}$ _____

9) $\frac{1}{6}$ _____

10) $\frac{2}{5}$ _____

Score out of ten →

3. A Whole One as a Fraction

Whole Ones or **Units** can also be expressed as fractions. If the numerator and the denominator are the same, the fraction is equal to one whole one.

Example: Show whole ones as fractions.

Numerator - How many parts?
Denominator - What type of parts?

Two-halves make a whole one;
Three-thirds make a whole one;
Four-quarters make a whole one.

$\frac{2}{2} = 1$ $\frac{3}{3} = 1$ $\frac{4}{4} = 1$

Exercise 4: 2 Express these whole ones as fractions:

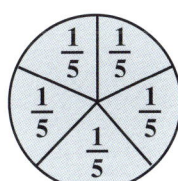 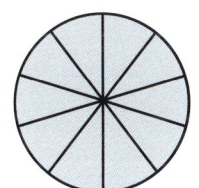 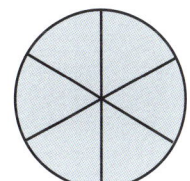 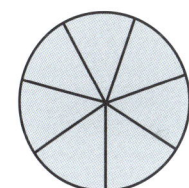

1) _____   2) _____   3) _____   4) _____

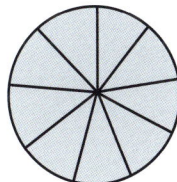 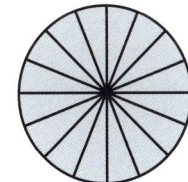 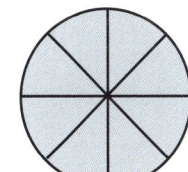 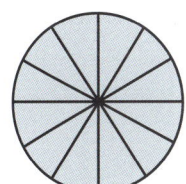

5) _____   6) _____   7) _____   8) _____

Express these fractions as whole ones:

9) $\frac{15}{15}$ = _____   10) $\frac{20}{20}$ = _____

Score

4. Proper Fractions

A **Proper Fraction** has a value that consists of less than one whole or one unit. It can be called a **Vulgar** or **Ordinary Fraction**.
A proper fraction has a smaller numerator and a larger denominator. It is '**bottom heavy**'.

Example: Represent $\frac{3}{4}$ as a proper fraction.

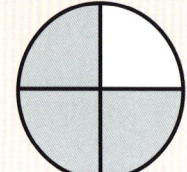

$\frac{3}{4}$ Smaller numerator
Larger denominator

Exercise 4: 3 Write the value of the shaded part:

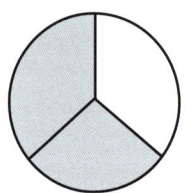 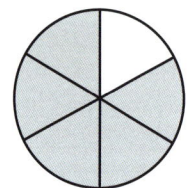 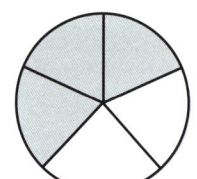 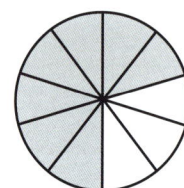

1) _____   2) _____   3) _____   4) _____

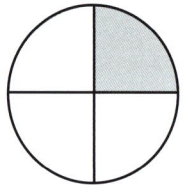 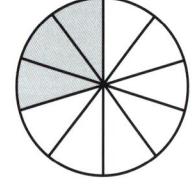 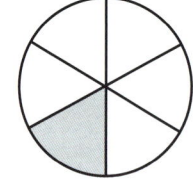 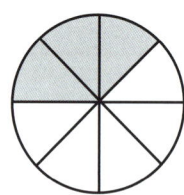

5) _____   6) _____   7) _____   8) _____

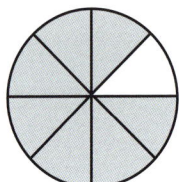 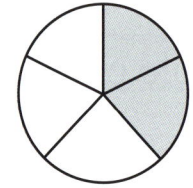

9) _____   10) _____

Score

Finding the value of the shaded fraction:

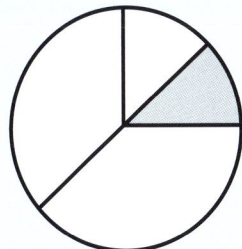 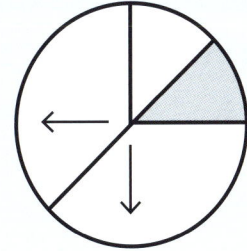 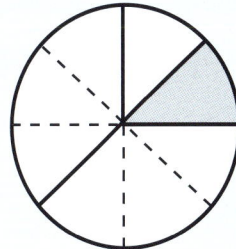

Lines are missing on this diagram, making it difficult to see what the fraction is.

Extend the existing lines across the circle. This shows it must be divided into eighths.

Draw in the other lines which are now obvious. The fractional part is **one-eighth**.

Exercise 4: 4 What is the shaded fraction? Score

1) 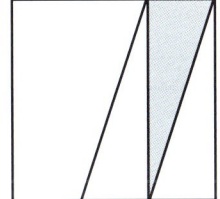 2) 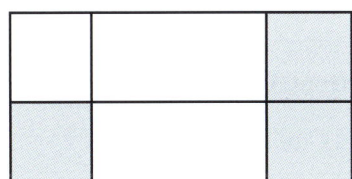 3)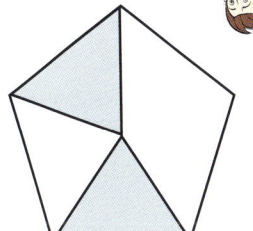

4) 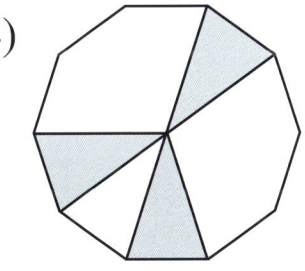 5) 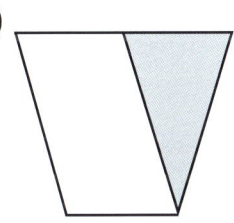 6)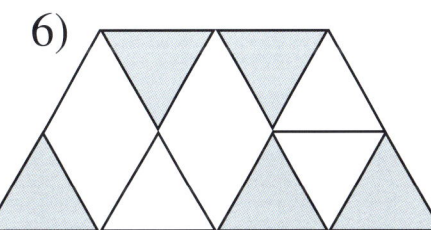

7) 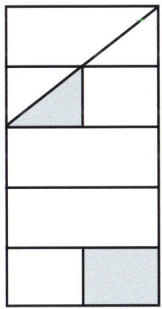 8) 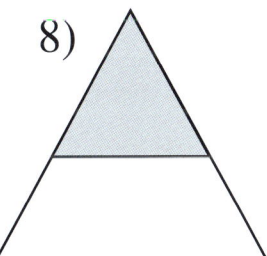 9)  10)

© 2006 Stephen Curran

5. Equal Fractions

Equal Fractions are also termed Equivalent Fractions. All three fractions have the same value:

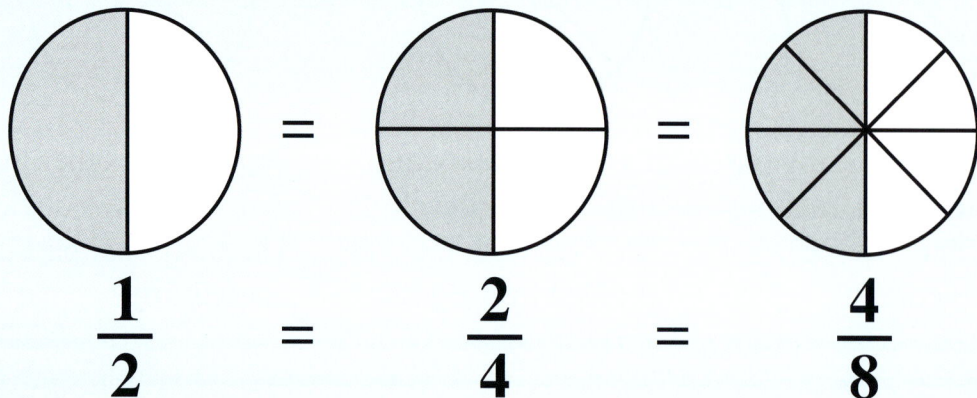

$$\frac{1}{2} = \frac{2}{4} = \frac{4}{8}$$

The relationship between the top and bottom half of an equal or equivalent fraction is always the same.

Example: Show a series of equal fractions. $\quad \frac{1}{2} = \frac{10}{20} = \frac{15}{30}$

The bottom half is twice the value of the top half.

Exercise 4: 5 Write the equivalent fraction:

1) $\frac{12}{16} = $ _____

2) $\frac{2}{5} = $ _____

3) _____ $= \frac{8}{12}$

4) _____ $= \frac{5}{8}$

5) ◯ = ◯   6) ◯ = ◯

   ___ = $\frac{3}{5}$ $\frac{4}{6}$ = ___

7) ◯ = ◯   8) ◯ = ◯

   $\frac{7}{8}$ = ___   ___ = $\frac{4}{12}$

9) ◯ = ◯   10) ◯ = ◯

   $\frac{4}{8}$ = ___   ___ = $\frac{2}{10}$

Fractions can be multiplied by the same number.

$\frac{1}{2} \xrightarrow{\times 2} = \frac{2}{4}$

Fractions can be divided by the same number.

$\frac{2}{4} \xrightarrow{\div 2} = \frac{1}{2}$

Exercise 4: 6 Write in the missing numbers:

1) $\frac{1}{4} \times \underline{} = \frac{4}{16}$

2) $\frac{5}{15} \div \underline{} = \frac{1}{3}$

3) $\frac{4}{5} \times \underline{} = \frac{20}{25}$

4) $\frac{6}{36} \div \underline{} = \frac{1}{6}$

5) $\dfrac{36}{42} \begin{array}{c}\div \underline{} \\ \div \underline{}\end{array} = \dfrac{6}{7}$ 6) $\dfrac{5}{8} \begin{array}{c}\times \underline{} \\ \times \underline{}\end{array} = \dfrac{20}{32}$

7) $\dfrac{72}{84} \begin{array}{c}\div \underline{} \\ \div \underline{}\end{array} = \dfrac{6}{7}$ 8) $\dfrac{3}{18} \begin{array}{c}\div \underline{} \\ \div \underline{}\end{array} = \dfrac{1}{6}$

9) $\dfrac{8}{10} \begin{array}{c}\times \underline{} \\ \times \underline{}\end{array} = \dfrac{72}{90}$ 10) $\dfrac{1}{3} \begin{array}{c}\times \underline{} \\ \times \underline{}\end{array} = \dfrac{25}{75}$

Score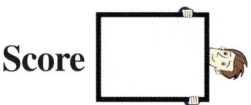

6. Simple Fractions

Simple Fractions are fractions in their **lowest terms**.

Example: Show a fraction in its lowest terms. $\dfrac{1}{2}$ This fraction cannot be expressed in any lower terms.

Simplifying fractions into their lowest terms.
Find a number (factor) that divides into the top and bottom of the fraction exactly with no remainder.

$\rightarrow$ Divide by **4**

$\dfrac{12 \div 4}{16 \div 4} = \dfrac{3}{4}$ Simplifying is usually shown like this. $\rightarrow$ $\dfrac{\cancel{12}^{\,3}}{\cancel{16}_{\,4}} = \dfrac{3}{4}$

Dividing by 2
If the top and bottom of the fraction are both **even** it can be divided by **2**.

Example: Simplify $\dfrac{16}{18}$

$\dfrac{16}{18} \begin{array}{c}\div 2 \\ \rightarrow \\ \div 2\end{array} \dfrac{\cancel{16}^{\,8}}{\cancel{18}_{\,9}} = \dfrac{8}{9}$

Dividing by 10
If the top and bottom of the fraction both end in **0**, it can be divided by **10** by simply removing the **0**s on the end.

Example: Simplify $\dfrac{20}{30}$

$\dfrac{20}{30} \begin{array}{c}\div 10 \\ \rightarrow \\ \div 10\end{array} \dfrac{\cancel{20}^{\,2}}{\cancel{30}_{\,3}} = \dfrac{2}{3}$

Exercise 4: 7   Simplify the following: Score

1) $\dfrac{3}{9}$ = _____

2) $\dfrac{8}{12}$ = _____

3) $\dfrac{5}{30}$ = _____

4) $\dfrac{15}{18}$ = _____

5) $\dfrac{8}{32}$ = _____

6) $\dfrac{25}{75}$ = _____

7) $\dfrac{56}{72}$ = _____

8) $\dfrac{60}{96}$ = _____

9) $\dfrac{72}{84}$ = _____

10) $\dfrac{72}{90}$ = _____

Example: Find the shaded fraction of equal value.

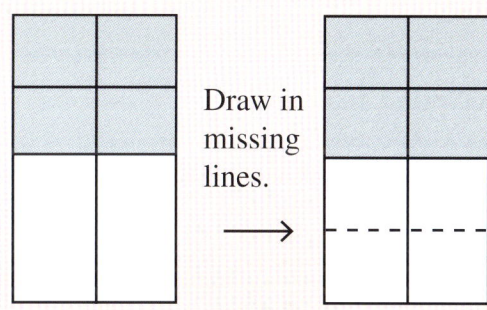

The fraction is $\dfrac{4}{8}$

Simplify $\dfrac{4^1}{8^2} = \dfrac{1}{2}$

Divide by 4

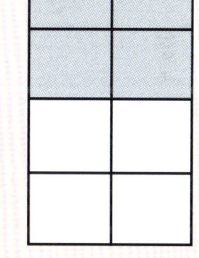

Exercise 4: 8   Write the fraction in lowest terms:

1)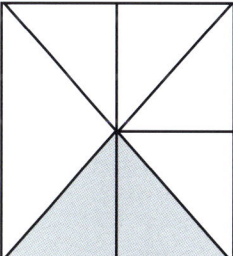

2)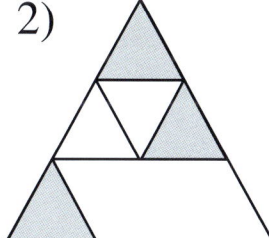

3)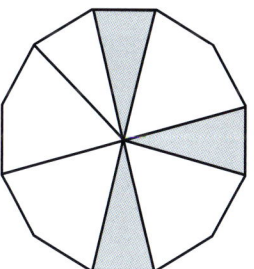

_____   _____   _____

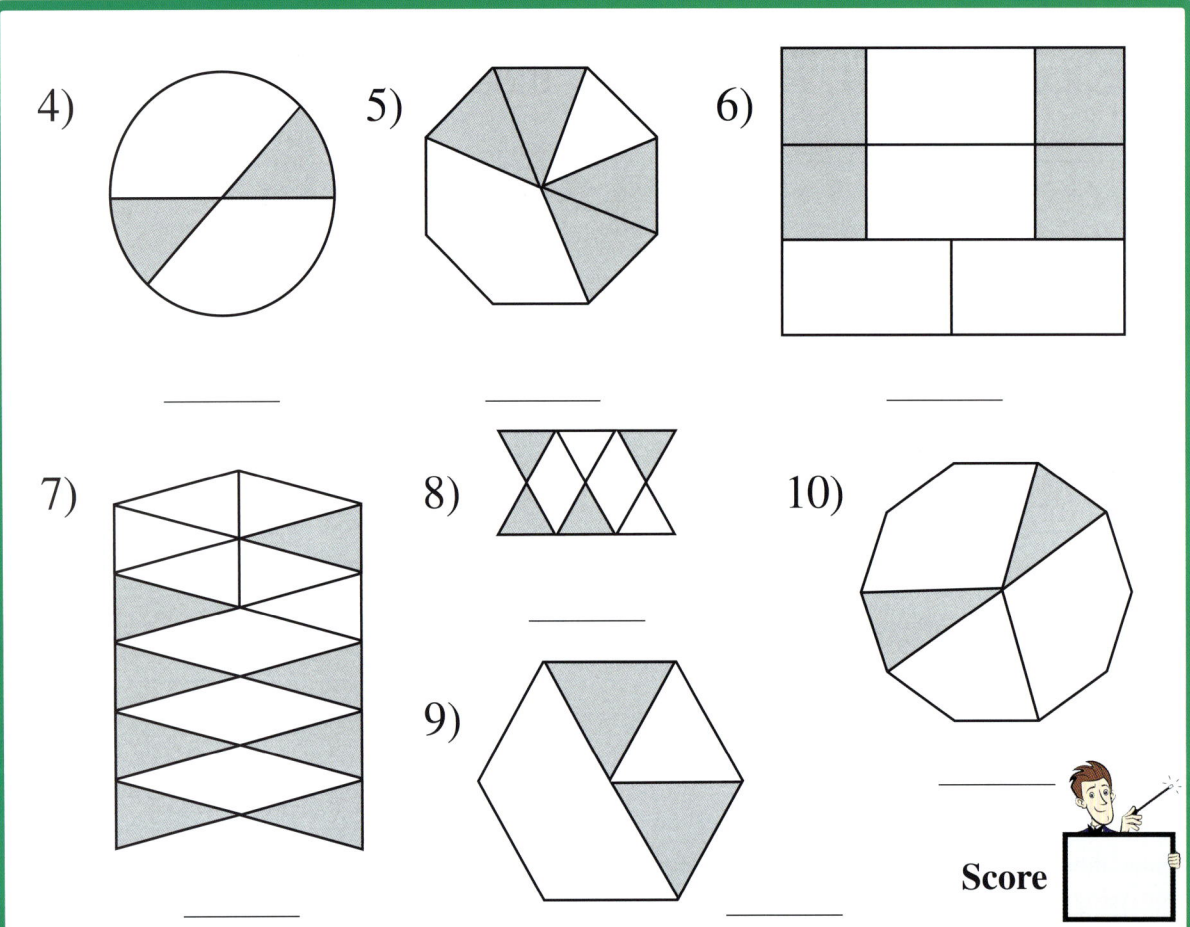

7. Complex Fractions

Complex Fractions are not in lowest terms.

Examples:
Show fractions in complex and simple forms.

$$\frac{8}{16} = \frac{4}{8} = \frac{2}{4} = \frac{1}{2}$$

Complex   Complex   Complex   Simple (lowest terms)

Fractions can be complicated by multiplying to infinity (forever) and by any combination of numbers.

$$\frac{1}{3} \times \frac{2}{2} = \frac{2}{6} \times \frac{3}{3} = \frac{6}{18} \times \frac{4}{4} = \frac{24}{72}$$

Multiply by **2**   Multiply by **3**   Multiply by **4**

Questions often appear with a missing number.

Example:

Write in the missing number. $\dfrac{3}{4} = \dfrac{?}{8}$

The multiplier is **2**.

$\dfrac{3}{4} \times 2 = \dfrac{6}{8}$
$\dfrac{3}{4} \times 2 = \dfrac{6}{8}$

Exercise 4: 9 Write the missing number:

1) $\dfrac{2}{3} = \dfrac{}{9}$

2) $\dfrac{1}{2} = \dfrac{6}{}$

3) $\dfrac{}{5} = \dfrac{16}{20}$

4) $\dfrac{5}{8} = \dfrac{}{24}$

5) $\dfrac{1}{3} = \dfrac{6}{}$

6) $\dfrac{}{15} = \dfrac{44}{60}$

7) $\dfrac{3}{4} = \dfrac{15}{}$

8) $\dfrac{3}{5} = \dfrac{}{30}$

9) $\dfrac{5}{} = \dfrac{15}{18}$

10) $\dfrac{7}{8} = \dfrac{}{40}$

8. Improper Fractions

Improper Fractions have a value of more than one unit. An improper fraction has a larger numerator and a smaller denominator. It is '**top heavy**'.

Example:

Show **seven-quarters** as an improper fraction.

$\dfrac{7}{4}$ Larger numerator

Smaller denominator

© 2006 Stephen Curran

Exercise 4: 10a Are the fractions proper or improper?

1) $\dfrac{4}{5}$ _____ 2) $\dfrac{9}{8}$ _____

3) $\dfrac{12}{8}$ _____ 4) $\dfrac{9}{10}$ _____

5) $\dfrac{20}{7}$ _____

Whole ones or units are always included in improper fractions. Therefore more than one whole one can be expressed as an improper fraction.

Example: Express these whole ones as an improper fraction.

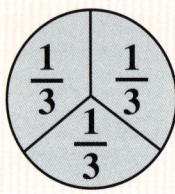 

There are **six-thirds**.

$6 \div 3 = \dfrac{6}{3}$

Numerator - How many shaded parts are there altogether?

Denominator - How many parts are in a whole?

Exercise 4: 10b Write as improper fractions:

6) _____ 7) _____

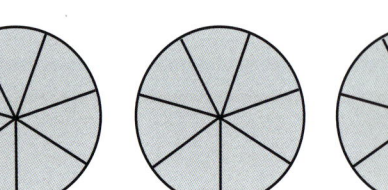 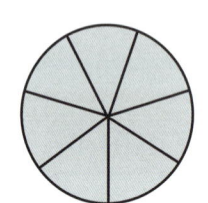

8) _____

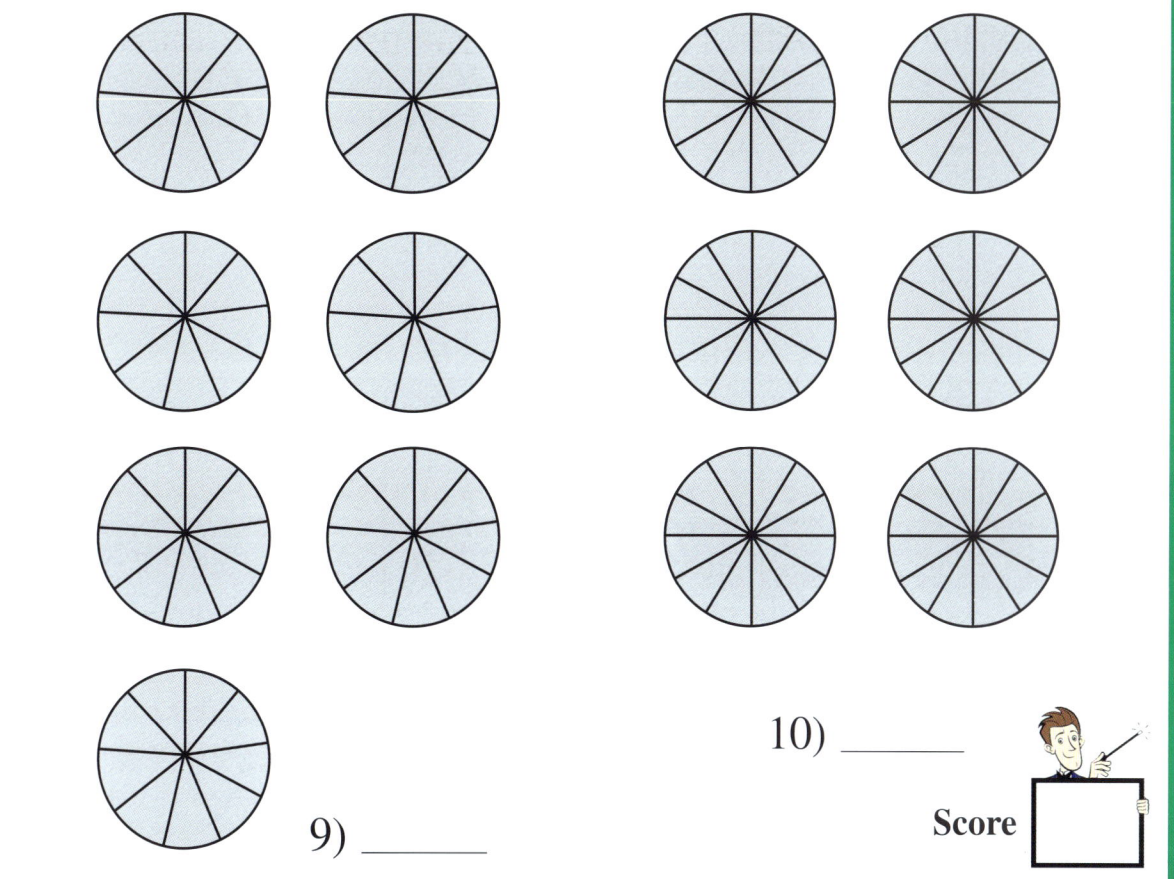

9) _____   10) _____

Score

Finding the value of an improper fraction:

For the **numerator** - Count the number of shaded parts.
For the **denominator** - It stays the same.

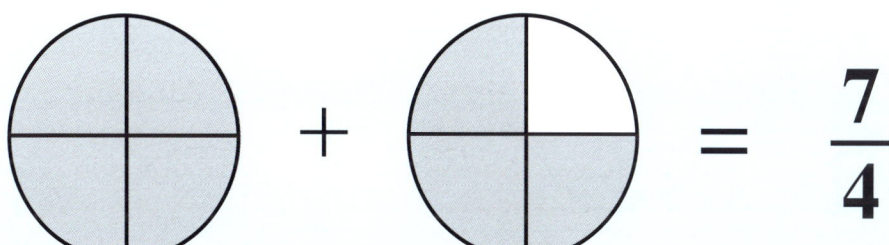

Exercise 4: 11 Write as improper fractions:

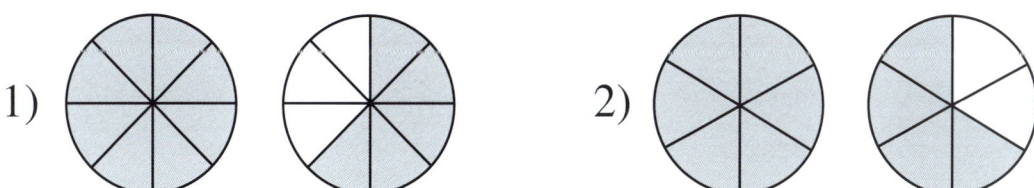

1) _____   2) _____

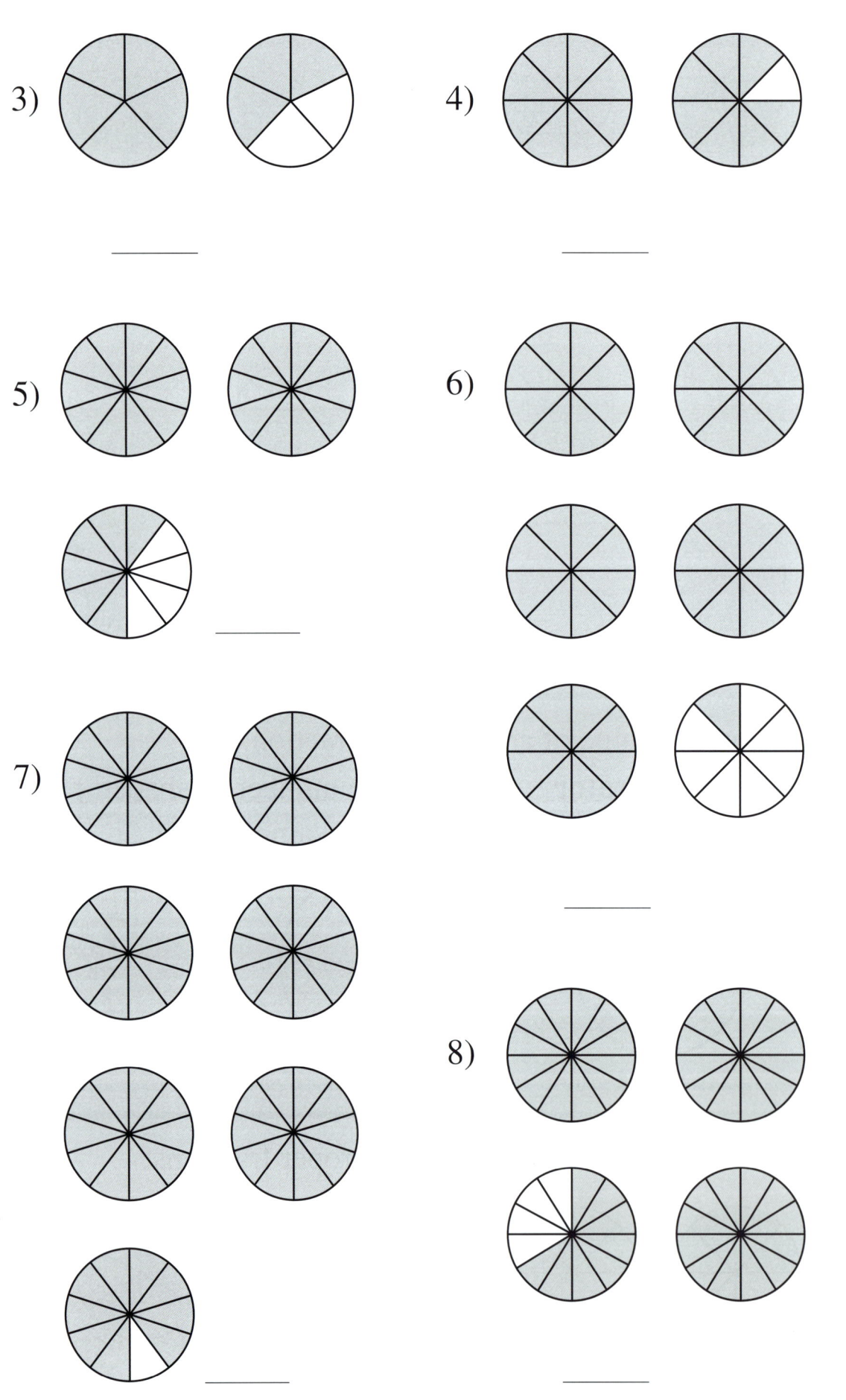

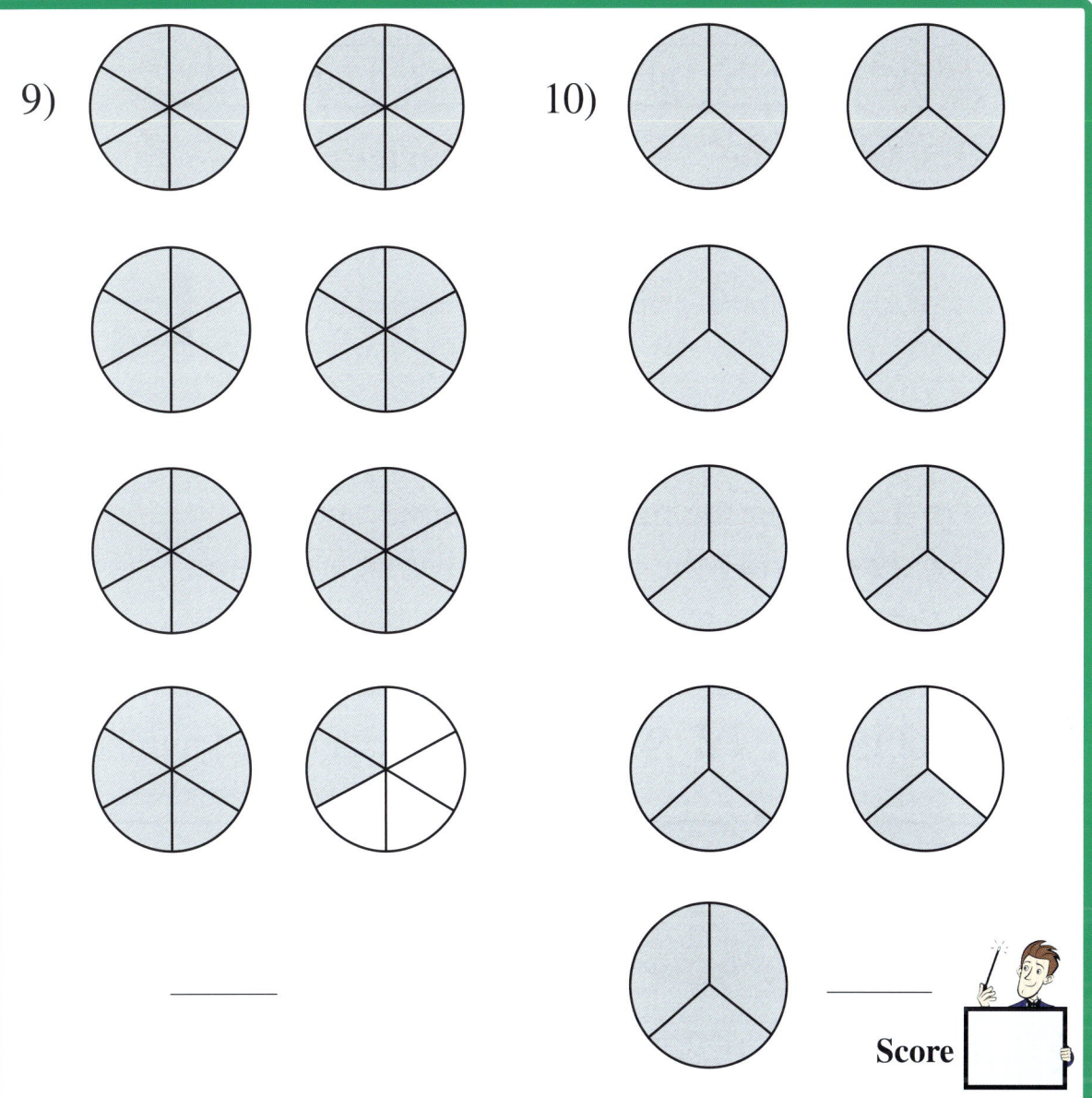

9. Mixed Numbers

Mixed Numbers are whole numbers and fractions combined together. The whole number is written first followed by the fraction.

A whole number + a fraction = a mixed number

Example: Show **one and three-quarters** as a mixed number.

One whole one ↗ $1\frac{3}{4}$ ↖ Three-quarters

Example: Find the value of this mixed number.

One whole one + Three-quarters

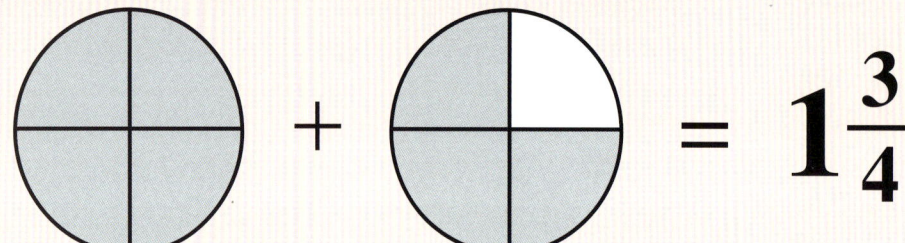

Mixed numbers are determined by:
- Counting the number of whole ones.
- Expressing the parts left over as a fraction.

Exercise 4: 12 Write the value as a mixed number:

1)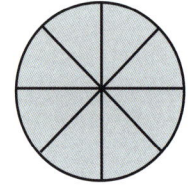

2)

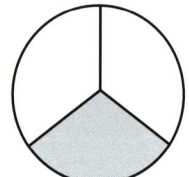

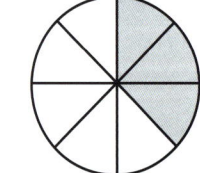

_____   _____

3)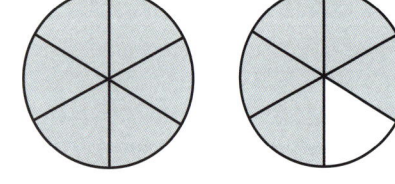

4)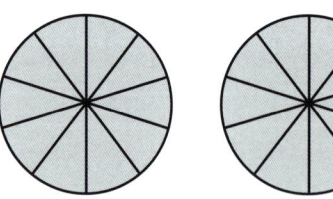

   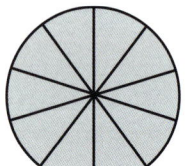 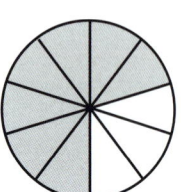

_____   _____

18   © 2006 Stephen Curran

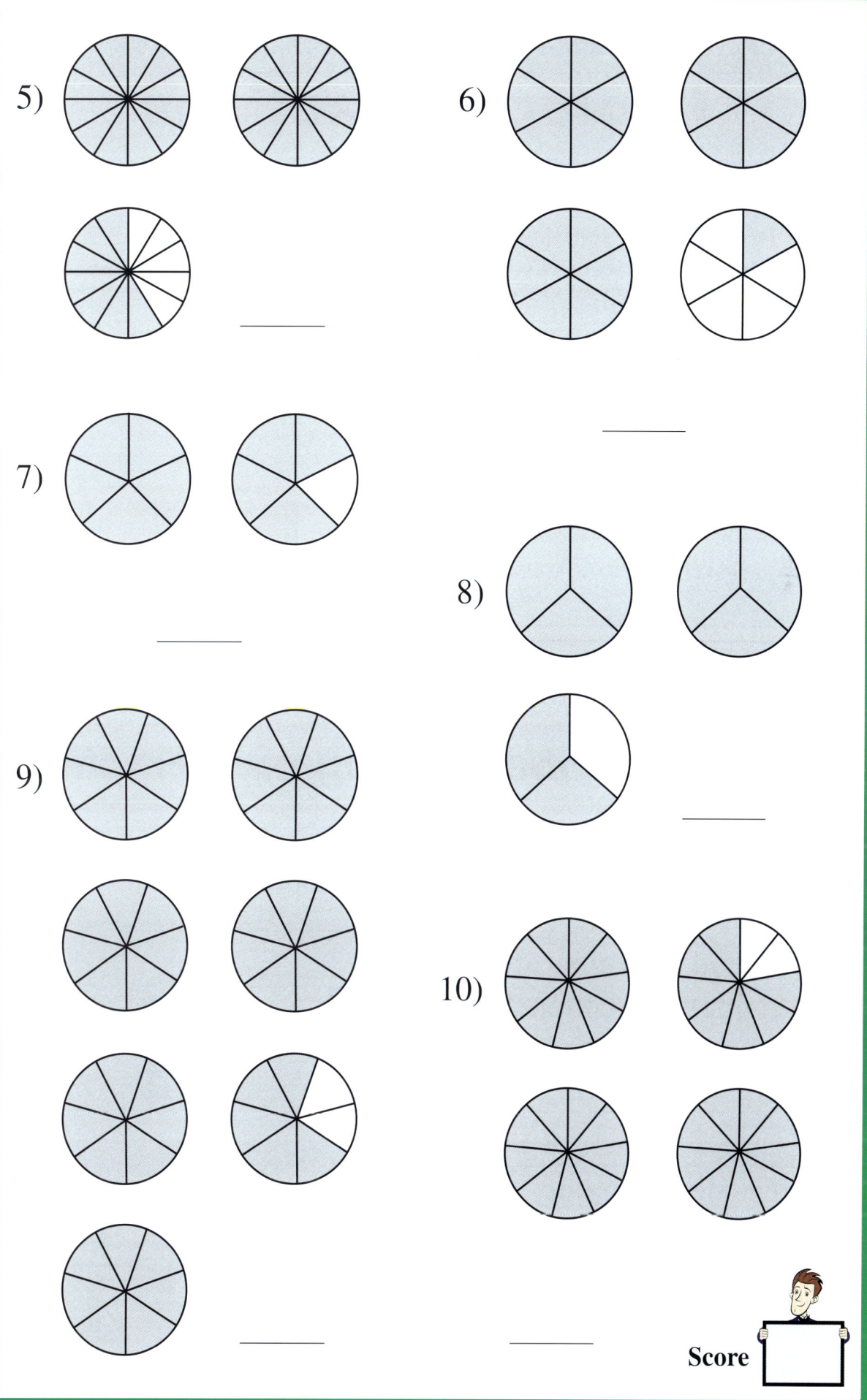

10. Mixed Numbers and Improper Fractions

Fractions can either be expressed as **Mixed Numbers** or **Improper Fractions**.

Example:

Express as a mixed number and an improper fraction.

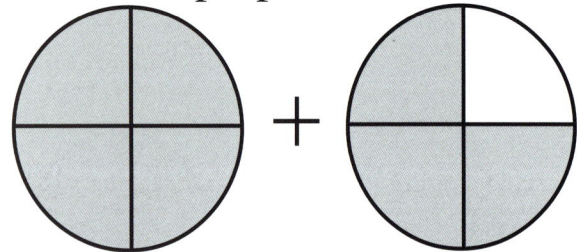

Mixed number | Improper fraction

$= 1\frac{3}{4}$ or $\frac{7}{4}$

Answers to problems are usually given in mixed numbers, but calculations are often done with improper fractions first.

a. Mixed Numbers to Improper Fractions

Example: Change $1\frac{3}{4}$ to an improper fraction.

To find the **numerator** multiply the bottom by the whole number then add the top to it.

$1 \times 4 = 4 \quad 4 + 3 = 7$

The **denominator** remains the same. It will be **4** as the fraction is in quarters.

Numerator $\quad \frac{7}{4}$
Denominator

Exercise 4: 13 Change to improper fractions:

1) $2\frac{1}{2}$ ____   2) $5\frac{3}{4}$ ____   3) $3\frac{2}{9}$ ____

4) $4\frac{2}{3}$ ____   5) $4\frac{3}{7}$ ____   6) $1\frac{5}{6}$ ____

7) $9\frac{5}{8}$ ____   8) $6\frac{4}{5}$ ____   9) $10\frac{5}{9}$ ____

10) $8\frac{7}{10}$ ____

Score ____

b. Improper Fractions to Mixed Numbers

Example: Change $\frac{7}{4}$ to a mixed number.

For the **whole number**:
Divide the top by the bottom.
$7 \div 4 = 1$ whole one

$\frac{7}{4}$ ↑ Divide

For the **fraction**:
Take the remainder of **3** and put it over the same denominator of **4** to make the fraction of:

$\frac{3}{4}$ **Three-quarters**

$1\frac{3}{4}$

Exercise 4: 14   Change to mixed numbers:

1) $\frac{4}{3}$ ____   2) $\frac{5}{2}$ ____   3) $\frac{7}{6}$ ____

4) $\dfrac{17}{4}$ _____   5) $\dfrac{16}{7}$ _____   6) $\dfrac{20}{5}$ _____

7) $\dfrac{25}{8}$ _____   8) $\dfrac{23}{10}$ _____   9) $\dfrac{19}{3}$ _____

10) $\dfrac{31}{9}$ _____

Score ☐

11. Lowest Common Denominators (LCD)

The **Lowest Common Denominator** or **Multiple** is the lowest number that all the denominators will divide into.

Examples 1-3: Name the lowest common denominators.

$\dfrac{1}{2}$ $\dfrac{3}{4}$ $\dfrac{2}{3}$ LCD **12**   The lowest number that **2**, **3** and **4** will divide into is **12**, so this is the lowest common denominator.
Clue - Use times tables.

$\dfrac{2}{3}$ $\dfrac{1}{6}$ LCD **6**   The LCD can be the largest denominator. In this case both **3** and **6** divide into the largest denominator of **6**.
Clue - The largest denominator.

$\dfrac{1}{3} \times \dfrac{3}{5}$ LCD **15**   The LCD can often be found simply by multiplying the denominators, as in this case. $3 \times 5 = 15$
Clue - Multiply the denominators.

Exercise 4: 15   Write the LCD of these fractions:

1) $\dfrac{1}{6}$ $\dfrac{2}{9}$ _____   2) $\dfrac{1}{4}$ $\dfrac{2}{3}$ _____   3) $\dfrac{5}{18}$ $\dfrac{5}{9}$ _____

4) $\dfrac{2}{3}$ $\dfrac{4}{9}$ _____   5) $\dfrac{3}{4}$ $\dfrac{4}{5}$ _____   6) $\dfrac{2}{5}$ $\dfrac{4}{7}$ _____

7) $\dfrac{2}{3}$ $\dfrac{9}{16}$ $\dfrac{5}{8}$ _____   8) $\dfrac{1}{4}$ $\dfrac{2}{5}$ $\dfrac{5}{6}$ _____

9) $\dfrac{2}{3}$ $\dfrac{5}{6}$ $\dfrac{1}{4}$ _____   10) $\dfrac{9}{10}$ $\dfrac{1}{5}$ $\dfrac{3}{4}$ _____

Score ☐

© 2006 Stephen Curran

12. The Four Rules of Fractions

Fractions can be added, subtracted, multiplied and divided. There are two basic methods, which must not be confused:
1. Adding and subtracting are linked by a common method.
2. Multiplying and dividing are linked by a common method.

13. Adding Fractions
a. Fractions with the Same Denominator

If the denominators are the same in both cases, add the numerators putting the answer over the same denominator.

Example: $\boxed{\dfrac{5}{9} + \dfrac{2}{9}}$ Add the numerators $5 + 2 = 7$ This gives the answer: $\dfrac{7}{9}$

Sometimes an addition will result in an improper fraction. This must be converted to a mixed number:

Example: $\boxed{\dfrac{6}{7} + \dfrac{5}{7}}$ Add the numerators $6 + 5 = 11$ This gives the answer: $\dfrac{11}{7} = 1\dfrac{4}{7}$

Exercise 4: 16a   Add the fractions:

1) $\dfrac{4}{11} + \dfrac{5}{11} = \underline{}$ 2) $\dfrac{5}{8} + \dfrac{1}{8} = \underline{}$ 3) $\dfrac{5}{13} + \dfrac{6}{13} = \underline{}$

4) $\dfrac{3}{4} + \dfrac{3}{4} = \underline{}$ 5) $\dfrac{4}{5} + \dfrac{3}{5} + \dfrac{2}{5} = \underline{}$

b. Fractions with Different Denominators

If fractions have **Different Denominators** another procedure is followed.

Example:
$\boxed{\dfrac{2}{3} + \dfrac{3}{4}}$

1. Find the lowest common denominator of **3** and **4**.

3 - 3, 6, 9, <u>12</u>
4 - 4, 8, <u>12</u>

© 2006 Stephen Curran

2. Change all the fractions to twelfths by multiplying the top and bottom of each fraction.

$$\frac{2 \times 4}{3 \times 4} = \frac{8}{12}$$

$$\frac{3 \times 3}{4 \times 3} = \frac{9}{12}$$

3. Draw a line and make **12** the denominator.

$$\frac{8+9}{12}$$

4. Add the numerators (not the denominator).

$$\frac{17}{12}$$

5. Divide to convert the improper fraction to a mixed number.

$$1\frac{5}{12}$$

Exercise 4: 16b   Add the fractions:

6) $\frac{1}{6} + \frac{3}{5}$

7) $\frac{5}{12} + \frac{1}{4}$

8) $\frac{5}{9} + \frac{1}{3}$

= _____

= _____

= _____

9) $\frac{3}{4} + \frac{4}{5} + \frac{7}{10}$

10) $\frac{4}{7} + \frac{5}{6} + \frac{1}{3}$

= _____

= _____

Score

c. Fractions with Mixed Numbers

Example:

$$3\frac{2}{3} + 2\frac{3}{4}$$

1. Add the whole numbers.
2. Find the lowest common multiple of both denominators.

3 - 3, 6, 9, <u>12</u>
4 - 4, 8, <u>12</u>   The LCM is **12**.

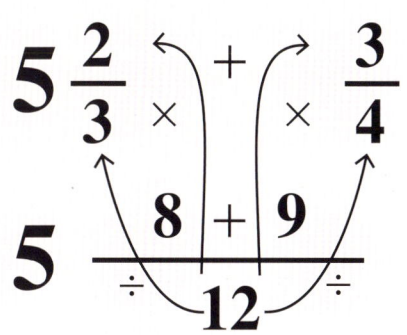

A quick way to find the new denominator - multiply the two existing denominators. (**3 × 4 = 12**) Make **12** the new denominator.

3. To find the new numerators, do the calculations shown.
   $12 ÷ 3 = 4 \quad 4 × 2 = 8$
   $12 ÷ 4 = 3 \quad 3 × 3 = 9$

| **An alternative calculation** can be done that achieves the same result. Use the multipliers to make twelfths. | Multiply each fraction to make twelfths. $\dfrac{2 × 4}{3 × 4} = \dfrac{8}{12} \quad \dfrac{3 × 3}{4 × 3} = \dfrac{9}{12}$ |

$5\dfrac{8 + 9}{12}$

4. Add the numerators.
   $8 + 9 = 17$

$5\dfrac{17}{12}$ ↑ Divide

5. This is an improper fraction. Convert to a mixed number.
   $17 ÷ 12 =$ **1** whole one and **5-twelfths** left over. $1\dfrac{5}{12}$

$5 + 1\dfrac{5}{12}$

6. Add the whole numbers.

$6\dfrac{5}{12}$

7. Does the fraction simplify? No number will divide into **5** and **12**.

Exercise 4: 17   Add the following fractions:

1) $2\dfrac{1}{2} + 3\dfrac{2}{3}$

2) $4\dfrac{1}{3} + 5\dfrac{3}{4}$

= _____

= _____

© 2006 Stephen Curran

3) $4\dfrac{2}{5} + 2\dfrac{3}{4}$

= _____

4) $9\dfrac{7}{8} + 7\dfrac{3}{4}$

= _____

5) $3\dfrac{2}{3} + 1\dfrac{7}{10}$

= _____

6) $1\dfrac{2}{3} + 2\dfrac{7}{9}$

= _____

7) $3\dfrac{1}{4} + \dfrac{8}{15} + \dfrac{2}{3}$

= _____

8) $1\dfrac{5}{16} + 2\dfrac{3}{8}$

= _____

9) $3\dfrac{5}{7} + 9\dfrac{4}{5}$

= _____

10) $6\dfrac{1}{8} + 4\dfrac{3}{5} + \dfrac{3}{4}$

= _____

Score

14. Subtracting Fractions

a. Fractions with the Same Denominator

It is the same method as addition, but subtract instead.

Example: $\boxed{\dfrac{7}{9} - \dfrac{5}{9}}$ Subtract the numerators $7 - 5 = 2$ This gives the answer: $\dfrac{2}{9}$

Exercise 4: 18a — Subtract the fractions:

1) $\dfrac{7}{11} - \dfrac{5}{11} = $ ___   2) $\dfrac{5}{8} - \dfrac{1}{8} = $ ___   3) $\dfrac{12}{13} - \dfrac{6}{13} = $ ___

4) $\dfrac{3}{4} - \dfrac{1}{4} = $ ___   5) $\dfrac{4}{5} - \dfrac{2}{5} - \dfrac{1}{5} = $ ___

b. Fractions with Different Denominators

Follow the same method as addition but subtract instead.

Example: $\boxed{\dfrac{2}{3} - \dfrac{2}{5}}$

1. Find LCM of **3** and **5**. $3 - 3, 6, 9, 12, \underline{15}$
   $5 - 5, 10, \underline{15}$

2. Change all the fractions to fifteenths by multiplying the top and bottom of each fraction.

   $\dfrac{2 \times 5}{3 \times 5} = \dfrac{10}{15}$

   $\dfrac{2 \times 3}{5 \times 3} = \dfrac{6}{15}$

3. Draw a line and make **15** the denominator. $\dfrac{10 - 6}{15}$

4. Subtract the numerators. $\dfrac{4}{15}$

Exercise 4: 18b — Subtract the fractions:

6) $\dfrac{5}{6} - \dfrac{3}{5} = $ ___   7) $\dfrac{11}{12} - \dfrac{2}{3} = $ ___   8) $\dfrac{8}{9} - \dfrac{5}{6} = $ ___

9) $\dfrac{5}{7} - \dfrac{1}{3} =$ _____   10) $\dfrac{7}{8} - \dfrac{3}{7} - \dfrac{1}{4} =$ _____
Score

c. Fractions with Mixed Numbers

Use the following method to subtract **Mixed Numbers**.

Example 1:

$$5\tfrac{1}{2} - 2\tfrac{1}{3}$$

1. Subtract the whole numbers.

2. Find the LCM of **2** and **3**.
   2 - 2, 4, <u>6</u>
   3 - 3, <u>6</u>   The LCM is **6**.

$$3\tfrac{1}{2} \tfrac{1}{3}$$

$$3\;\dfrac{3 - 2}{6}$$

3. Calculation.
   $6 \div 2 = 3 \qquad 3 \times 1 = 3$
   $6 \div 3 = 2 \qquad 2 \times 1 = 2$

$$3\;\dfrac{3-2}{6}$$

4. Subtract the numerators.

$$3\tfrac{1}{6}$$

5. Is it improper and will it simplify? Not in this case.

Exercise 4: 19a   Subtract the following fractions:

1) $5\tfrac{1}{2} - 1\tfrac{2}{5}$ 2) $4\tfrac{3}{4} - 1\tfrac{5}{8}$

= _____   = _____

3) $3\frac{2}{5} - 1\frac{1}{8}$ 4) $6\frac{2}{3} - 3\frac{2}{5} - \frac{1}{10}$

= _____   = _____

5) $8\frac{3}{4} - 6\frac{1}{3} - \frac{1}{6}$ 6) $6\frac{3}{4} - 2\frac{3}{8}$

= _____   = _____

d. Subtractions with Borrowing

In this example the first mixed number is of greater value than the second mixed number so they can be subtracted.

Example 2:

$$3\frac{1}{5} - 1\frac{3}{4}$$

Smaller fraction ↓   Bigger fraction ↓

$3\frac{1}{5} - 1\frac{3}{4}$

$\overset{20+}{\cancel{2}^{1}} \frac{4-15}{20}$

However, the second fraction is bigger than the first so **Borrowing** will be required.

1. Subtract the whole numbers.
2. Find the LCM.
3. Do the calculation.
4. Borrow a whole one.

   4 − 15 cannot be done. Cross out the **2** and put **1**.

   The whole one = $\frac{20}{20}$ and is put into the fraction.

© 2006 Stephen Curran

$1\frac{9}{20}$ 5. Add in and subtract.
         6. Improper/simplify? No.

Exercise 4: 19b   (Questions 7-10 require borrowing.)

7) $11\frac{1}{6} - 3\frac{4}{9}$ 8) $1\frac{7}{20} - \frac{14}{15}$

= _____   = _____

9) $11\frac{2}{9} - 5\frac{3}{4}$ 10) $91\frac{1}{2} - 16\frac{7}{8}$

Score

= _____   = _____

15. Two Rule Fractions (+ & −)

Some fraction sums involve addition and subtraction.

Example: $\boxed{\frac{4}{5} + \frac{3}{4} - \frac{1}{3}}$

1. Change to sixtieths.   2. Add and subtract in the order of the sum.

$\frac{4^{\times 12}}{5_{\times 12}} + \frac{3^{\times 15}}{4_{\times 15}} - \frac{1^{\times 20}}{3_{\times 20}}$ $\frac{48}{60} + \frac{45}{60} - \frac{20}{60} = \frac{73}{60} = 1\frac{13}{60}$

Exercise 4: 20   Calculate the following:

Score

1) $\frac{1}{6} + \frac{2}{3} - \frac{5}{8} =$ _____   2) $\frac{9}{10} - \frac{1}{4} + \frac{1}{5} =$ _____

3) $1\frac{3}{4} + 1\frac{3}{5} - \frac{1}{2} = $ _____ 4) $\frac{3}{5} + \frac{5}{6} - \frac{1}{10} = $ _____

5) $2\frac{1}{2} + 1\frac{1}{3} - \frac{4}{9} = $ _____ 6) $3\frac{1}{5} - \frac{3}{4} + \frac{3}{10} = $ _____

7) $2\frac{7}{10} - 1\frac{1}{4} - \frac{3}{5} = $ _____ 8) $\frac{5}{6} - \frac{2}{3} + \frac{1}{8} = $ _____

9) $3\frac{2}{3} + \frac{1}{6} - 1\frac{3}{4} = $ _____ 10) $2\frac{1}{2} - \frac{7}{16} - \frac{3}{4} = $ _____

16. Multiplying Fractions

a. Proper Fractions

Multiplying Proper Fractions involves multiplying out the top and bottom of each fraction.

Example: Multiply out the fractions.

$\boxed{\dfrac{1}{3} \times \dfrac{4}{5}}$ $\dfrac{1}{3} \times \dfrac{4}{5}$ $\begin{array}{l} 1 \times 4 = \\ 3 \times 5 = \end{array} \dfrac{4}{15}$

Exercise 4: 21a   Answer the following:

1) $\dfrac{1}{5} \times \dfrac{3}{4} = $ _____ 2) $\dfrac{5}{7} \times \dfrac{2}{11} = $ _____ 3) $\dfrac{2}{9} \times \dfrac{4}{5} = $ _____

b. Cancelling Proper Fractions

Sometimes it is possible to **Cancel** the fractions down before multiplying them out.

Example 1: $\boxed{\dfrac{4}{9} \times \dfrac{15}{16}}$

1. Cancel (cross-divide). Find a number (factor) that divides both numbers diagonally.

$$\frac{^1\cancel{4}}{_3\cancel{9}} \times \frac{\cancel{15}^5}{\cancel{16}^4}$$

   9 and **15** both divide by **3**. $9 \div 3 = 3;\ 15 \div 3 = 5$
   4 and **16** both divide by **4**. $4 \div 4 = 1;\ 16 \div 4 = 4$

   Now check to simplify each fraction.

2. Multiply out the fractions.
   $1 \times 5 = 5 \qquad 3 \times 4 = 12$

   $$\frac{1}{3} \times \frac{5}{4}$$

3. Will the fraction simplify? Not in this case.

Answer: $\dfrac{5}{12}$

It is possible to cancel more than two fractions:

Example 2:

$$\boxed{\frac{9}{10} \times \frac{5}{6} \times \frac{2}{3}}$$

Stage 1: $\dfrac{9}{_2\cancel{10}} \times \dfrac{^1\cancel{5}}{_3\cancel{6}} \times \dfrac{\cancel{2}^1}{3}$

Stage 2: $\dfrac{^3\cancel{9}}{2} \times \dfrac{1}{_1\cancel{3}} \times \dfrac{1}{3}$

Stage 3: $\dfrac{^1\cancel{3}}{2} \times \dfrac{1}{1} \times \dfrac{1}{\cancel{3}^1}$

It is easier to see the process of cancelling in stages as shown above on the right.

$$\dfrac{^{1\,3}\cancel{9}}{_2\cancel{10}} \times \dfrac{^1\cancel{5}}{_{1\,3}\cancel{6}} \times \dfrac{\cancel{2}^1}{\cancel{3}^1} = \dfrac{1}{2}$$

Exercise 4: 21b   Answer the following:

4) $\dfrac{3}{4} \times \dfrac{2}{3} =$ _____   5) $\dfrac{5}{6} \times \dfrac{3}{10} =$ _____   6) $\dfrac{2}{5} \times \dfrac{5}{8} =$ _____

7) $\dfrac{5}{12} \times \dfrac{4}{15} \times \dfrac{3}{4} =$ _____   8) $\dfrac{8}{9} \times \dfrac{9}{10} \times \dfrac{5}{6} =$ _____

9) $\dfrac{6}{7} \times \dfrac{2}{3} =$ _____   10) $\dfrac{4}{5} \times \dfrac{5}{14} \times \dfrac{4}{5} =$ _____

Score

c. Mixed Numbers

Example:

$$4\frac{1}{6} \times 1\frac{1}{15}$$

1. Convert **Mixed Numbers** to improper fractions.

Convert

$$4^{+1}_{\times 6} \times 1^{+1}_{\times 15}$$

2. Cancel (cross-divide). Find a number (factor) that will divide both numbers diagonally across the two fractions.

Cancel

$$\frac{{}^5 25}{{}_3 6} \times \frac{16^{\,8}}{15^{\,3}}$$

25 and **15** both divide by **5**.
$25 \div 5 = 5$; $15 \div 5 = 3$

16 and **6** both divide by **2**.
$16 \div 2 = 8$; $6 \div 2 = 3$

Check to see if each fraction can be simplified further.

Multiply

$$\frac{5}{3} \times \frac{8}{3}$$

3. Multiply out the fractions; both the numerators and denominators.

$$\frac{40}{9}$$ Divide

4. Is it an improper fraction? Yes, so divide the fraction to return to a mixed number.

$$4\frac{4}{9}$$

5. Will it simplify? No, as the fraction is in its lowest terms.

Exercise 4: 22 Multiply the following fractions:

1) $3\frac{1}{4} \times 1\frac{1}{3}$

2) $1\frac{3}{10} \times \frac{5}{8}$

= _____

= _____

3) $1\frac{1}{2} \times 7$ 4) $2\frac{1}{2} \times 2\frac{2}{5}$

= _____   = _____

5) $\frac{3}{5} \times \frac{2}{3}$ 6) $\frac{3}{8} \times 56$

= _____   = _____

7) $5\frac{1}{2} \times \frac{3}{8}$ 8) $4\frac{2}{5} \times \frac{5}{11}$

= _____   = _____

9) $\frac{8}{11} \times 1\frac{1}{3}$ 10) $\frac{1}{8} \times 1\frac{3}{5}$

Score

= _____   = _____

17. Dividing Fractions
a. Proper Fractions

Dividing Proper Fractions involves two extra stages.

Example: $\boxed{\dfrac{7}{8} \div \dfrac{7}{16}}$

1. The second fraction is inverted.
2. The division sign is changed to multiplication.

$\dfrac{7}{16} \xrightarrow{\text{Invert}} \dfrac{16}{7}$

1. Turn the second fraction (the divisor) upside down (invert).

$$\frac{^1 7}{_1 8} \times \frac{16\,^2}{7\,_1}$$

$$\frac{1}{1} \times \frac{2}{1}$$

$$\frac{2}{1} \;\; \text{Divide} = 2$$

2. Change the division sign to a multiplication sign.
$$\frac{7}{8} \div \frac{7}{16} \rightarrow \frac{7}{8} \times \frac{16}{7}$$
3. Cancel the fractions as normal.
4. Multiply out the fractions.
5. Is it an improper fraction? Yes.
6. Will it simplify? No.

A useful way to remember this method is: leave it, change it, flip it.

	Leave It	Change It	Flip It
	$\frac{7}{8}$	$\div$	$\frac{7}{16}$
	$\downarrow$	$\downarrow$	$\downarrow$
	$\frac{7}{8}$	$\times$	$\frac{16}{7}$

Exercise 4: 23   Divide the following fractions:

1) $\frac{3}{4} \div \frac{1}{2}$ 2) $\frac{5}{6} \div \frac{2}{3}$ 3) $\frac{2}{5} \div \frac{4}{5}$

= ___   = ___   = ___

4) $\frac{3}{4} \div \frac{6}{8}$ 5) $\frac{5}{6} \div \frac{10}{12}$ 6) $\frac{3}{5} \div \frac{9}{10}$

= ___   = ___   = ___

7) $\frac{6}{7} \div \frac{15}{21}$ 8) $\frac{8}{9} \div \frac{2}{3}$ 9) $\frac{5}{12} \div \frac{5}{6}$

= ___   = ___   = ___

10) $\frac{4}{5} \div \frac{16}{25}$

= ___

Score

© 2006 Stephen Curran

b. Mixed Numbers

The method is the same as multiplying except for stage 2.

Example: $2\frac{1}{4} \div 1\frac{7}{8} \longrightarrow \dfrac{2\frac{1}{4}}{1\frac{7}{8}}$

This is exactly the same sum.

If the sum is given in this format, set it out in the original way.

1. Convert to improper fractions.

$\dfrac{9}{4} \div \dfrac{15}{8}$

Change to × — Invert the 2nd Fraction

2. Three Rules of Division:
   a. Turn the second fraction upside down (invert). This is called the **Reciprocal** of the original fraction.
   b. Change the division sign to a multiply sign.
   c. Proceed as a normal multiplication.

$\dfrac{\overset{3}{\cancel{9}}}{\underset{1}{\cancel{4}}} \times \dfrac{\overset{2}{\cancel{8}}}{\underset{5}{\cancel{15}}}$

3. Cancel (cross-divide).

$\dfrac{3}{1} \times \dfrac{2}{5}$

4. Multiply out the fractions.

$\dfrac{6}{5}$ Divide

5. Is it an improper fraction? Yes, so divide the fraction.

$1\frac{1}{5}$

6. Will it simplify? The fraction is already in lowest terms.

Exercise 4: 24 Divide the following fractions:

1) $3\frac{1}{5} \div 1\frac{7}{25}$ 2) $3\frac{1}{3} \div 1\frac{2}{3}$

= _____   = _____

3) $1\frac{1}{2} \div 3$ 4) $\frac{5}{8} \div 1\frac{2}{3}$

= _____   = _____

5) $3\frac{1}{2} \div 1\frac{1}{4}$ 6) $7\frac{1}{2} \div 3$

= _____   = _____

7) $5\frac{1}{2} \div \frac{4}{5}$ 8) $\frac{3}{4} \div \frac{1}{5}$

= _____   = _____

9) $\dfrac{1\frac{1}{2}}{\frac{2}{3}}$ This question should be set out like this before commencing: $1\frac{1}{2} \div \frac{2}{3}$ 10) $\dfrac{2\frac{2}{9}}{1\frac{2}{3}}$

Score

= _____   = _____

18. Two Rule Fractions (× & ÷)

Some fraction sums involve multiplication and division.

Example: Solve the following: $\frac{2}{3} \times \frac{5}{8} \div \frac{5}{9}$ The same sum can be written like this. $\dfrac{\frac{2}{3} \times \frac{5}{8}}{\frac{5}{9}}$

1. Invert divisions and change ÷ to × $\frac{2}{3} \times \frac{5}{8} \div \frac{5}{9}$ 2. Cancel $\frac{^1\cancel{2}}{_1\cancel{3}} \times \frac{^1\cancel{5}}{_4\cancel{8}} \times \frac{\cancel{9}^3}{\cancel{5}^1} = \frac{3}{4}$

Exercise 4: 25 Calculate the following: Score

1) $1\frac{1}{3} \div 2 \div \frac{7}{15}$ = ___

2) $\dfrac{3\frac{9}{10} \div 6\frac{1}{2}}{\frac{7}{15}}$ = ___

3) $5\frac{1}{2} \times \frac{9}{10} \div 4\frac{2}{5}$ = ___

4) $1\frac{2}{3} \times \frac{7}{10} \div 2\frac{4}{5}$ = ___

5) $\dfrac{3\frac{1}{3} \times \frac{4}{5}}{5\frac{1}{3}}$ = ___

6) $2\frac{2}{3} \times \frac{1}{2} \div 1\frac{3}{5}$ = ___

7) $\frac{3}{8} \times \frac{3}{8} \times \frac{4}{9}$ = ___

8) $1\frac{5}{6} \times \frac{3}{5} \div 8\frac{1}{4}$ = ___

9) $2\frac{1}{2} \div 1\frac{1}{3} \div 2\frac{1}{12}$ = ___

10) $\frac{1}{4} \times \frac{2}{3} \div \frac{5}{9}$ = ___

19. Four Rule Fractions (+ − × ÷)

The **BIDMAS** acronym gives the Order of Operations.
Brackets, **I**ndices, **D**ivision, **M**ultiplication, **A**ddition and **S**ubtraction
Do the brackets first, then do ÷ or ×, then do + or − .

a. With Brackets

If there are brackets, always do the sums inside first.

Example: Show the order of operations in:

$3\frac{2}{5} \div \left(2\frac{1}{2} + \frac{1}{3}\right)$ The same sum can be written like this without the brackets. $\dfrac{3\frac{2}{5}}{2\frac{1}{2} + \frac{1}{3}}$

	Operation 1		Operation 2
Add	$2\frac{1}{2} + \frac{1}{3} = 2\frac{5}{6}$	Divide	$3\frac{2}{5} \div 2\frac{5}{6} = 1\frac{1}{5}$

Exercise 4: 26a   Calculate the following:

1) $5\frac{5}{6} \div (3\frac{1}{2} + \frac{2}{3}) =$ ___

2) $\dfrac{\frac{1}{4} + \frac{1}{7}}{3\frac{3}{10}} =$ ___

3) $\dfrac{2\frac{4}{5} \div 2\frac{1}{2}}{1\frac{2}{5} \times \frac{1}{3}} =$ ___

4) $1\frac{4}{5} \times (2\frac{1}{4} - \frac{7}{12}) =$ ___

5) $(4\frac{1}{2} - 1\frac{3}{4}) \div 7\frac{1}{3} =$ ___

b. Without Brackets

When there are no brackets, ensure that you do the ÷ or × sums first, then do the + or − sums next.

Example: Show the order of operations in: $2\frac{1}{4} \times 2\frac{5}{6} - 1\frac{2}{3}$

	Operation 1		Operation 2
Multiply	$2\frac{1}{4} \times 2\frac{5}{6} = 6\frac{3}{8}$	Subtract	$6\frac{3}{8} - 1\frac{2}{3} = 4\frac{17}{24}$

Exercise 4: 26b   Calculate the following:

6) $3\frac{1}{7} \div 1\frac{3}{8} + \frac{1}{2} =$ ___

7) $\frac{1}{2} + 3\frac{3}{5} \times \frac{5}{8} =$ ___

8) $1\frac{1}{7} \times 2\frac{3}{4} \div 4 =$ ___

9) $5\frac{1}{3} \times \frac{5}{8} - 3\frac{1}{3} =$ ___

10) $4\frac{3}{4} - 1\frac{3}{10} \times 2\frac{1}{2} =$ ___

Score

20. Fractional Parts

Example: Find $\frac{7}{8}$ of **96**. This sum can be done in two ways.

1. a. Find the value of $\frac{1}{8}$. Divide the whole number by the denominator. **96 ÷ 8 = 12**

   b. Find the value of $\frac{7}{8}$. Multiply by the numerator. **7 × 12 = 84**

2. Multiplying can be termed as 'of'. $\frac{7}{{}_1 8} \times \frac{\cancel{96}^{12}}{1} = \frac{7 \times 12}{1 \times 1} = 84$

Exercise 4: 27a Find the fractional part:

1) $\frac{2}{3}$ of **387**. _____

2) $\frac{5}{7}$ of **273**. _____

3) $\frac{4}{5}$ of **540**. _____

4) $\frac{8}{11}$ of **341**. _____

5) $\frac{5}{6}$ of **240**. _____

Example: Find the whole when $\frac{4}{5}$ is **84**. There are two methods again.

1. a. Divide the whole number by the numerator to find how big each part is.   **84 ÷ 4 = 21**

   b. Multiply the part by the denominator to find the size of the whole number.   **21 × 5 = 105**

2. It can be done by dividing fractions.

   ('is' can be treated as ÷)

   $$\frac{84}{1} \div \frac{4}{5} \longrightarrow \frac{\overset{21}{\cancel{84}}}{1} \times \frac{5}{\cancel{4}_1}$$

   $$\frac{21 \times 5}{1 \times 1} = 105$$

Exercise 4: 27b Find the whole when:

6) $\frac{4}{5}$ is **120**. _____

7) $\frac{6}{7}$ is **420**. _____

8) $\frac{5}{8}$ is **625**. _____

9) $\frac{5}{7}$ is **130**. _____

10) $\frac{9}{20}$ is **270**. _____

Score

21. Decimals and Fractions
a. Converting Decimals to Fractions

Example: Convert **1.375** to a mixed number.

1. Draw a decimal table and place the value in it.

O	t	h	th
1 •	3	7	5

1 whole one and 375 thousandths or $\longrightarrow 1\frac{375}{1000}$

2. Simplify $1\frac{\cancel{375}^{15}}{\cancel{1000}_{40}} \longrightarrow 1\frac{\cancel{15}^{3}}{\cancel{40}_{8}} \longrightarrow 1\frac{3}{8}$

Divide by **25**   Divide by **5**

Therefore **1.375** = $1\frac{3}{8}$

Exercise 4: 28 Change to mixed number fractions: Score

1) 0.5 = _____ 2) 0.125 = _____
3) 3.36 = _____ 4) 4.675 = _____
5) 0.7 = _____ 6) 8.15 = _____
7) 6.8 = _____ 8) 3.2 = _____
9) 5.75 = _____ 10) 4.625 = _____

b. Converting Fractions to Decimals

Example: Convert $1\frac{3}{8}$ to a decimal.

The whole number stays the same.
Divide the fraction: $3 \div 8 = 0.375$

$$8 \overline{) 3.0^60^40} \quad 0.375$$

Therefore $1\frac{3}{8} = 1.375$

Exercise 4: 29 Change to decimals, correct to 3 d.p.:

1) $\frac{5}{8}$ = _____ 2) $\frac{2}{3}$ = _____
3) $3\frac{1}{6}$ = _____ 4) $3\frac{2}{5}$ = _____
5) $4\frac{1}{7}$ = _____ 6) $\frac{1}{8}$ = _____
7) $3\frac{4}{9}$ = _____ 8) $2\frac{7}{8}$ = _____
9) $\frac{4}{7}$ = _____ 10) $2\frac{4}{5}$ = _____

22. Fractions in Size Order

Method 1

Change into fractions of the same type.

Example: Arrange the fractions in size order, smallest first. $\quad \dfrac{5}{12} \quad \dfrac{3}{4} \quad \dfrac{1}{2} \quad \dfrac{2}{3}$

1. The denominators will all divide into **12** (LCD is **12**), so make them all into twelfths by multiplying.

$\dfrac{5}{12}\qquad$ Multiply by 3: $\dfrac{3}{4} \times \dfrac{3}{3} = \dfrac{9}{12}\qquad$ Multiply by 6: $\dfrac{1}{2} \times \dfrac{6}{6} = \dfrac{6}{12}\qquad$ Multiply by 4: $\dfrac{2}{3} \times \dfrac{4}{4} = \dfrac{8}{12}$

2. Arrange in size order.

$\dfrac{5}{12} \quad \dfrac{6}{12} \quad \dfrac{8}{12} \quad \dfrac{9}{12}$

↓ ↓ ↓ ↓

3. Convert ordered fractions back to original form.

$\dfrac{5}{12} \quad \dfrac{1}{2} \quad \dfrac{2}{3} \quad \dfrac{3}{4}$

Exercise 4: 30a

Make the fractions have the same denominator:

Which of these fractions are bigger?

1) $\dfrac{5}{6} \quad \dfrac{4}{5}$ ____

2) $\dfrac{2}{3} \quad \dfrac{3}{4}$ ____

3) $\dfrac{5}{6} \quad \dfrac{6}{7}$ ____

Put in size order, smallest first:

4) $\dfrac{7}{8} \quad \dfrac{3}{4} \quad \dfrac{13}{16}$

5) $\dfrac{9}{20} \quad \dfrac{1}{5} \quad \dfrac{3}{10} \quad \dfrac{5}{8}$

= ____ ____ ____   = ____ ____ ____ ____

Method 2

Change into decimals first.

Example: Arrange the fractions in size order, smallest first. $\frac{5}{12}$ $\frac{3}{4}$ $\frac{1}{2}$ $\frac{2}{3}$

1. Change the fractions you know into decimals. $\frac{1}{2} = 0.5$ $\frac{3}{4} = 0.75$

2. Divide the other fractions to obtain decimal values.

$\frac{5}{12}$ ↑ Divide $12\overline{)5.000}$ (0.416) $\frac{2}{3}$ ↑ Divide $3\overline{)2.0^20}$ (0.66)

$\frac{5}{12} = 0.42$ $\frac{2}{3} = 0.\dot{6}$

3. Arrange in size order. 0.42 0.5 0.$\dot{6}$ 0.75
   ↓ ↓ ↓ ↓

4. Convert ordered decimals back to fractions. $\frac{5}{12}$ $\frac{1}{2}$ $\frac{2}{3}$ $\frac{3}{4}$

Exercise 4: 30b

Change the fractions into decimals first:

Score

Which of these fractions are smaller?

6) $\frac{4}{5}$ $\frac{3}{4}$ ____   7) $\frac{4}{7}$ $\frac{2}{3}$ ____   8) $\frac{3}{5}$ $\frac{5}{8}$ ____

Put in size order, largest first:

9) $\frac{9}{16}$ $\frac{3}{4}$ $\frac{3}{8}$ 10) $\frac{1}{2}$ $\frac{3}{5}$ $\frac{2}{3}$ $\frac{5}{6}$

= ____ ____ ____   = ____ ____ ____ ____

> Questions sometimes mix fractions and decimals.
> If possible convert the decimals to fractions as this is more straightforward. When there is no LCM all the fractions must be converted to decimals as in most questions below.

Exercise 4: 31 Which is smallest? Score

Convert to fractions.
1) 0.6 $\frac{3}{10}$ 0.15 _____

Convert to decimals.
2) $\frac{7}{11}$ 0.57 $\frac{3}{8}$ _____

Convert to fractions.
3) $\frac{9}{20}$ 0.56 $\frac{3}{4}$ _____

Convert to decimals.
4) 1.1 $\frac{7}{8}$ 0.95 _____

Which is largest?

Convert to decimals.
5) 0.47 $\frac{4}{9}$ 0.76 _____

Convert to decimals.
6) 0.44 $\frac{3}{5}$ 0.53 _____

Convert to decimals.
7) $\frac{7}{12}$ 0.61 $\frac{5}{8}$ _____

Convert to fractions.
8) $\frac{7}{10}$ 0.78 $\frac{3}{5}$ _____

Convert to decimals in both cases.

9) Put in size order, smallest first. 0.95 $\frac{5}{8}$ 0.59 = _____ _____ _____

10) Put in size order, largest first. $\frac{1}{12}$ 0.13 $\frac{1}{9}$ = _____ _____ _____

23. Fraction Problems

> Fractions often appear in Problem Solving questions.

Example:

Paul is $9\frac{1}{2}$ years old and his grandfather is 76 years old. Express Paul's age as a fraction of his grandfather's age.

1. Multiply $9\frac{1}{2}$ and 76 by 2 to eliminate the fraction.
$9\frac{1}{2} \times 2 = 19$ $76 \times 2 = 152$

2. Express 19 and 152 as a fraction and then simplify. $\frac{19^1}{152^8} = \frac{1}{8}$

Exercise 4: 32 Solve the following problems:

1) Pavneet walks **3** miles on a sponsored walk of **15** miles. What fraction of the walk did he complete? ____

2) John gave Priya $\frac{1}{3}$ and Navin $\frac{1}{4}$ of his birthday cake. What fraction of the cake did that leave for John? ____

3) Larry drank $\frac{4}{5}$ of $\frac{3}{4}$ of $\frac{5}{6}$ of his cola can. What fraction of the cola was left? (Remember 'of' is ×.) ____

4) Two identical chocolate bars were equally divided between **3** children. What fraction did each receive? ____

5) Alex is $1\frac{1}{2}$ times older than his sister, Philippa. If Alex is **9** years old, how old is Philippa? ____ years

6) Find the sum of $1\frac{2}{3}$, $3\frac{4}{5}$ and $2\frac{3}{4}$. ____

7) Multiply the sum of $5\frac{3}{10}$ and $4\frac{1}{2}$ by $1\frac{3}{7}$. ____

8) Divide $2\frac{5}{6}$ by the sum of $2\frac{1}{2}$ and $\frac{1}{3}$. ____

9) Subtract $\frac{5}{6}$ from the product of $\frac{4}{5}$ and $2\frac{7}{8}$. ____

10) Add $3\frac{5}{6}$ to the quotient of $1\frac{4}{7}$ and $2\frac{3}{4}$. ____

Score

24. Fraction Boxes

Some fraction problems can be solved with a **Fraction Box**.

Example:

Paula is given a new reading book that has **96** pages. She reads $\frac{3}{8}$ of the book. How many pages does she still have to read?

1. The missing fraction. This fraction completes the whole one.

$$\frac{3}{8} + \boxed{\frac{5}{8}} = \frac{8}{8}$$

Pages Read	Pages to Read
Given Fraction $\frac{3}{8}$ (12)	Missing Fraction $\frac{5}{8}$ (12)
Amount 3 × 12 = 36 **36**	Amount 5 × 12 = 60 **60**
Total 36 + 60 = 96 **96**	Value - One Part $\frac{1}{8}$ = 12

2. The value of one part. What is **one** part of a total of **8** parts?

   Divide **96** by the denominator **8**.

   $\frac{1}{8}$ of **96** = **12**

3. Calculate the amounts.

   Multiply **12** by the numerators.

   3 × **12** = **36** pages
   5 × **12** = **60** pages

   Paula still has 60 pages to read.

For the total number just add the amounts together.

Exercise 4: 33a   Solve the following:

Given Fraction	Missing Fraction
Amount	Amount
Total	One Part

1) $\frac{3}{7}$ of the children on a trip are boys. **28** are girls. How many children went on the trip?
   _____ children

2) In a class of **27** children, $\frac{1}{3}$ of them enjoy playing computer games. How many do not enjoy the games? _____ children

3) A school brochure has **72** pages. $\frac{3}{8}$ of the pages contain photographs. How many pages do not contain any photographs?
   _____ pages

© 2006 Stephen Curran

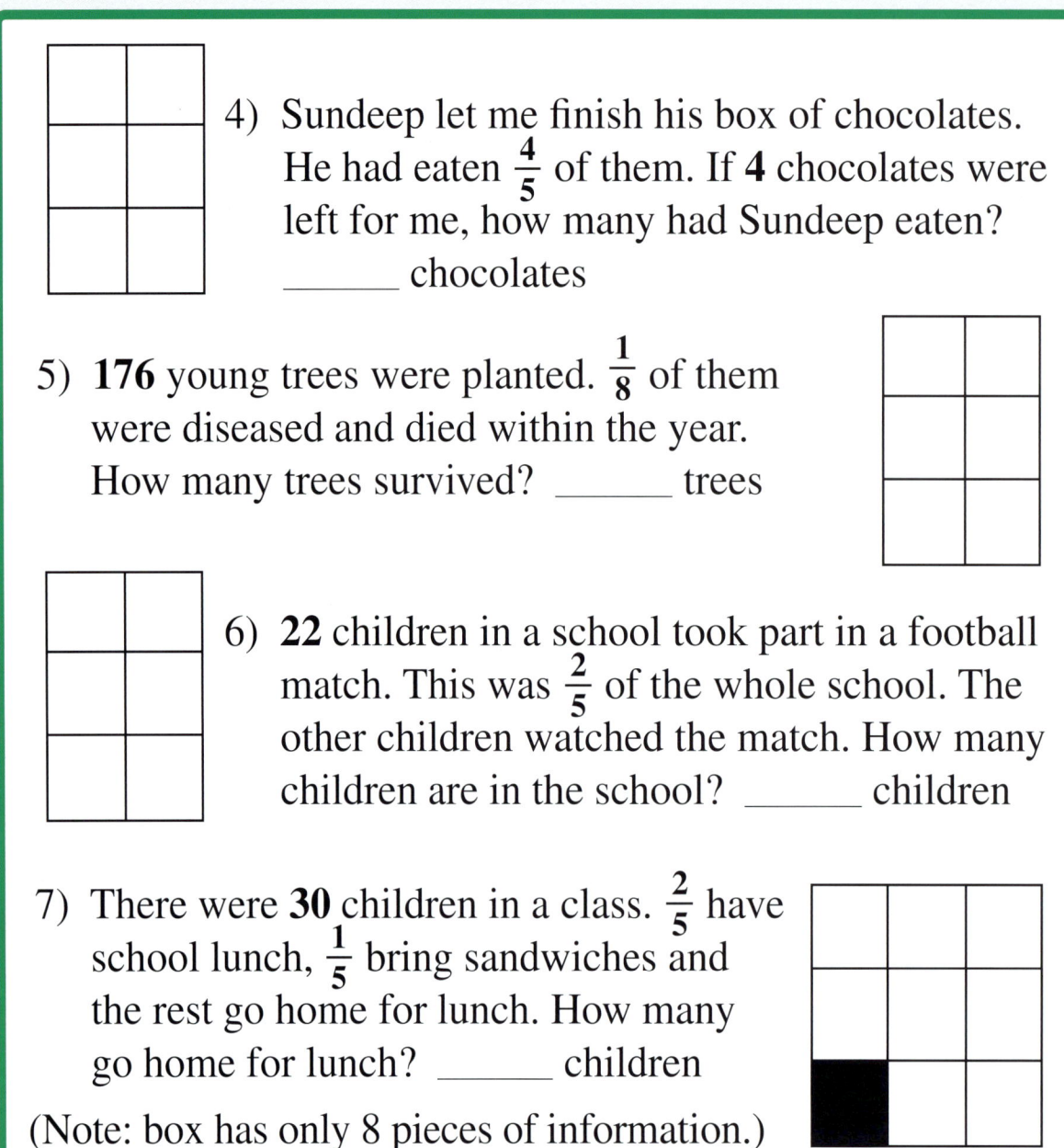

4) Sundeep let me finish his box of chocolates. He had eaten $\frac{4}{5}$ of them. If **4** chocolates were left for me, how many had Sundeep eaten? _____ chocolates

5) **176** young trees were planted. $\frac{1}{8}$ of them were diseased and died within the year. How many trees survived? _____ trees

6) **22** children in a school took part in a football match. This was $\frac{2}{5}$ of the whole school. The other children watched the match. How many children are in the school? _____ children

7) There were **30** children in a class. $\frac{2}{5}$ have school lunch, $\frac{1}{5}$ bring sandwiches and the rest go home for lunch. How many go home for lunch? _____ children

(Note: box has only 8 pieces of information.)

Variations on the fraction box question.

Example: Some sweets were shared out. Susan got $\frac{2}{5}$ of them. She gave **6** to Peter and had **12** left. How many sweets were there altogether?

There are two parts to this question.

1. Find the original amounts that people had or what they are left with.
2. Use the fraction box to solve the problem.

1. Original amounts.

 Add **6** and **12** to find the $\frac{2}{5}$ that Susan had at first.

 Susan had **18** sweets originally so $\frac{2}{5} = 18$

2. Fraction box.

Fraction Given	Fraction Missing
$\frac{2}{5}$	$\frac{3}{5}$
Amount $2 \times 9 = 18$ **18**	Amount $3 \times 9 = 27$ **27**
Total $18 + 27 = 45$ **45**	One Part $45 \div 5 = 9$ $\frac{1}{5} = 9$

a. Fill in the missing fraction.
 $\frac{2}{5} + \boxed{\frac{3}{5}} = \frac{5}{5}$

b. Find the value of one part.
 If $\frac{2}{5} = 18$ then $\frac{1}{5} = 9$

c. Calculate the other amount.
 $3 \times 9 = 27$

d. Find the total.
 $18 + 27 = 45$

There were 45 sweets altogether.

Exercise 4: 33b Solve the following:

Given Fraction	Missing Fraction
Amount	Amount
Total	One Part

8) When $\frac{4}{9}$ of a certain number is reduced by **19**, the result is **21**. What is the number?
 The number is _____ .

9) When some mints were shared John received $\frac{5}{12}$ of them. He gave **6** to Sunil and had **14** left. How many mints were there altogether?
 _____ mints

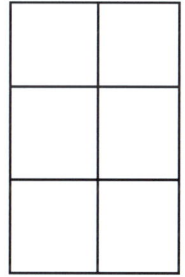

10) Peter swaps $\frac{2}{5}$ of his **35** stickers for **9** of Lucy's. How many has Peter got now?
 _____ stickers

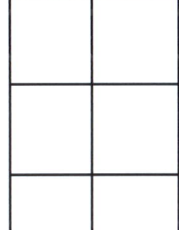

Do in this order:
1. Fraction box.
2. Calculate what Peter is left with.

Score ☐

25. Fraction Number Lines

Number Lines often utilise fractions. The fractions must be changed to the most appropriate unit for working.

Example:

Write in $\frac{13}{32}$ and its decimal value on the number line.

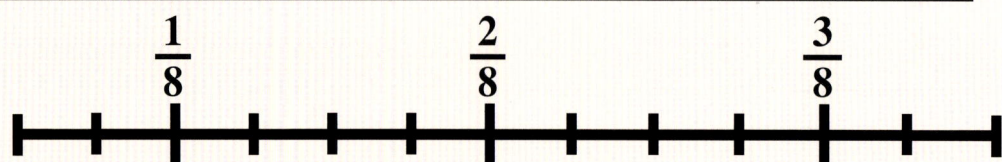

1. Convert the given fractions to 32nds (multiply by **4**).
2. Place $\frac{13}{32}$ on the number line (line units are 32nds).
3. Divide the fraction to find a decimal. $13 \div 32 \approx 0.41$

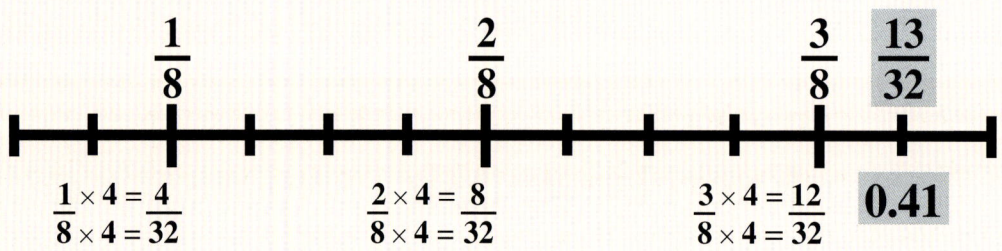

Exercise 4: 34 Calculate the following: Score ☐

Write as fractions.

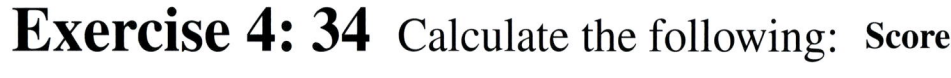

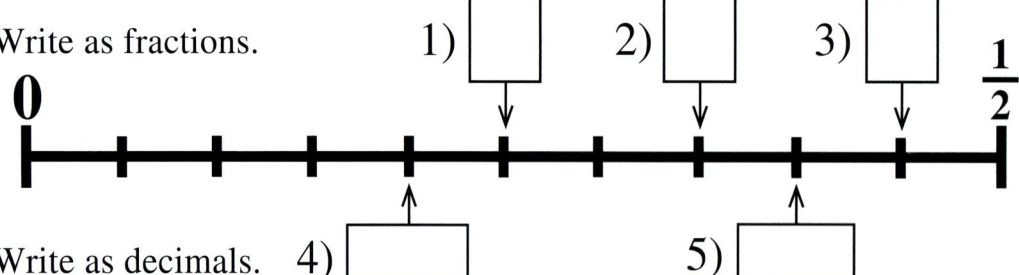

Write as decimals.

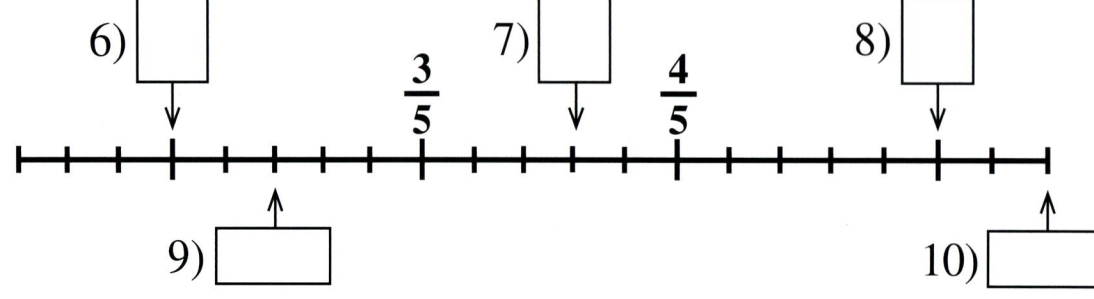

26. More Fraction Problems

Exercise 4: 35   Answer the following: **Score**

1) How much would each child get if **six and a half** cakes were shared among **four** children? (Divide.) _____ cakes

2) What is **three-quarters** of **four-ninths**? (Multiply.) _____

3) $11\frac{1}{6} - 3\frac{3}{7}$

   = _____

4) $4\frac{5}{8} + 5\frac{9}{16}$

   = _____

5) $4\frac{2}{3} \div 5\frac{4}{9}$

   = _____

6) $4\frac{1}{8} \times 7\frac{3}{11}$

   = _____

7) A boy scored **66** points on the first stage of a computer game. This was $\frac{3}{5}$ of his final score. What was his score once he had completed the game? _____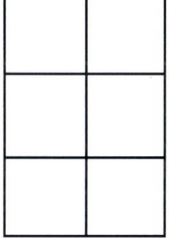

8) Simplify the following fractions:

   a) $\frac{60}{96}$ _____   b) $\frac{14}{70}$ _____   c) $\frac{21}{56}$ _____

9) Convert these improper fractions into mixed numbers:

   a) $\frac{72}{50}$ _____   b) $\frac{24}{10}$ _____   c) $\frac{50}{16}$ _____

10) Convert these mixed numbers into improper fractions:

    a) $6\frac{8}{9}$ _____   b) $3\frac{6}{7}$ _____   c) $2\frac{9}{10}$ _____

Chapter Five
MONEY AND COSTS
1. Units of Currency

Most money systems (currencies) in the world are based on the Tens Number System (units of ten).
- The United Kingdom uses pounds and pence. There are one hundred pence to one pound. The £ sign is based on the letter 'L'. It stands for libra, which means pounds in Latin.
- Countries in the European Union, excluding the UK, use the euro (€) and cent as a **Unit of Currency**. There are one hundred cents to the euro.
- The USA uses dollars ($) and cents. There are one hundred cents to the dollar.

2. Pounds and Pence

Multiply by **100** to change pounds to pence. (Move decimal point 2 places to the right.) Example: £1.63 = 163p

Divide by **100** to change pence to pounds. (Move decimal point 2 places to the left.) Example: 953p = £9.53

Exercise 5: 1

Score

Change to pence:
1) £6.30 = _____
2) £0.41 = _____
3) £8.95 = _____
4) £5.69 = _____
5) £9.02 = _____

Change to pounds:
6) 76p = _____
7) 1540p = _____
8) 153p = _____
9) 7p = _____
10) 18p = _____

3. Money Calculations

Remember: work in either pounds or pence.
Use rules for adding, subtracting, multiplying and dividing decimals (see Maths Workbook 1).

Exercise 5: 2 Set out and calculate: Score

1) £3.44 + 69p + £7.56
   = £ _____

2) £7.84 − 97p
   = £ _____

3) 599p + £4.37 + £0.88
   = £ _____

4) £8.07 − 596p
   = £ _____

5) 67 × £5.32   = £ _____

6) 56 × 730p   = £ _____

7) £7.70 ÷ 1.4   = £ _____

8) 656p ÷ 16   = £ _____

9) £66.73 × 9   = £ _____

10) £78.80 ÷ 8   = £ _____

4. Money Problems

Money Problems make use of the Four Rules of Decimals.

Example: Peter is given **£7.50** at Christmas and a further **£12.50** on his birthday from his aunt. His younger brother Jonathan receives **half** as much on both occasions from the same aunt. How much does Jonathan receive altogether?

Add   £7.50 + £12.50 = £20.00
Divide   £20.00 ÷ 2 = £10.00
Jonathan receives £10.00.

© 2006 Stephen Curran

Exercise 5: 3 Calculate the following:

1) Mrs Dhawal's supermarket bill comes to **£14.63**. At the checkout she buys her child sweets, which cost **£1.26**. What new amount does she pay? (Add.) £ _____

2) Anne spends **£63.92** on **8** new CDs in a sale. What was the cost of each CD? (Divide.) £ _____

3) Jane does a paper round and earns **£7.50** a week. She saves for a MP3 player that costs **£40**. How many weeks will she need to work to buy it? (Divide.) _____ weeks

4) Manpreet has a **£1** coin, a **50p** coin, **three 20p** coins, **two 10p** coins and **four 2p** coins. How much does she have? (Add.) £ _____

5) Computer games cost **£39.99**. How much would **4** of these games cost? (Multiply.) £ _____

6) Paul buys **4** sets of football stickers. He is given **36p** change from a **£1** coin. How much did each set cost? (Subtract and divide.) _____ p

7) A holiday in Spain costs **£225** per person. There is a **£55** reduction for children. How much would it cost Mr and Mrs Carter to go to Spain and take their two children? (Add, subtract and multiply.) £ _____

8) Dominic's parents buy him a new school jumper in a sale at half price. The original cost of the jumper was **£15.50**. How much change do they get from a **£20** note? (Divide and subtract.) £ _____

9) Year 5 go on an adventure holiday. There are **63** children and each child has to pay **£135**. How much must be collected in total? (Multiply.) £ _____

10) The cinema charges **£5.50** for adults and **£4.25** for children. It costs **£2.50** for a large bag of sweets and **75p** each for lemonade. How much will it cost Mr and Mrs Stenning to take their three children if they buy one bag of sweets and everyone has a drink of lemonade? (Multiply and add.) £ _____

Score

5. Costs

If you are given the **Cost** of a number of items, it is possible to find the cost of a different number of items.

Example: | **10** buns cost **£2.50**. Find the cost of **6** buns.

1. Find the cost of **one** bun (divide): $250p \div 10 = 25p$
2. **Six** buns will cost (multiply): $6 \times 25p = 150p$

The standard method is to multiply fractions.

1. Express the cost of **one** bun and the new number as fractions.

   The cost of one bun expressed as a fraction.   Multiplied by the new number expressed as a fraction.

2. Simplify/cancel.

$$\frac{^{25}\cancel{250}}{^{1}\cancel{10}} \times \frac{6}{1}$$

3. Multiply. $25 \times 6 = 150p$ or **£1.50**

Therefore 6 buns will cost £1.50.

Exercise 5: 4   Calculate the following:

1) **5kg** of oranges cost **£2.40**. What will **10kg** cost? (Simplify/cancel/multiply out.)
   10kg will cost £ _____ $\quad \frac{240}{5} \times \frac{10}{1}$

2) **150** packs of sweets weigh **9kg**. What will **250** similar packs of sweets weigh?
   250 packs will weigh _____ kg. $\quad \frac{9}{150} \times \frac{250}{1}$

© 2006 Stephen Curran

3) If eggs cost **90p** for **3 dozen** (12 to a dozen), what would: **7 dozen** eggs cost? £ _____   **1 egg** cost? _____ p

4) If stickers cost **30p** for **50**, how much would it cost to buy **450** stickers? £ _____

5) If **8lb** of tomatoes cost **96p**, how much would **12lb** of tomatoes cost? £ _____

6) If I can fill **26** glasses from **4** bottles of lemonade, how many glasses can **10** bottles fill? _____ glasses

7) **7** ice creams cost **91p**. How much will **11** ice creams cost? £ _____

8) **5** people have an Indian takeaway and pay a total of **£17.50**. What will **three** people have to pay for the same meal? £ _____

9) **30** metres of wood flooring cost **£450**. How much will **75** metres cost? £ _____

10) **7** litres of pineapple juice cost **£5.60**. How much will **12** litres cost? £ _____

Score

6. Currency Conversions

Conversion between one currency and another can be solved in a similar way to costs.

Example: On holiday, Peter buys a book for **6** dollars. He calculates this has cost him **£2.40**. What would a **21** dollar T-shirt cost in pounds?

1. Find the conversion factor or exchange rate ($ to £).

   Divide **240** (pence) ÷ **6** (dollars) = **40** so $\boxed{1 \text{ dollar} = 40p}$

2. Multiply to find the cost of the new item.
   The T-shirt would cost: **21 × 40p = £8.40**

   $\dfrac{240}{6} \times \dfrac{21}{1}$ = **£8.40** or same as costs calculation.

Exercise 5: 5 Calculate the following:

Score

1-3) Mr Bannerjee wants to take a business trip to India. Before he leaves he goes to the bank to buy some currency. He receives **8,000** Indian rupees for **100** British pounds.
What is the exchange rate? £1 = _____ rupees
At the bank he exchanges **£450** for _____ rupees.
On his return he exchanges **1,000** rupees for £ _____.

4-6) Whilst in the USA Mrs Jones buys a new handbag for **12** dollars and some earrings for **5** dollars. She works out that the new handbag costs **£4.80** and the earrings cost **£2.00**. How much in pounds would it cost her
to buy: a new blouse at **7** dollars?   £ _____
a new pair of shoes at **16** dollars?   £ _____
a necklace at **50** dollars?   £ _____

7-8) Mr Porter buys a meal in Denmark for **300** kroner which will convert to **£30**. How much would it cost him to buy: perfume at **750** kroner?   £ _____
a watch for **2,000** kroner?   £ _____

9-10) If **£1** equals **1.5** euros, convert the following:
£25 into euros. € _____   **€200** into pounds. £ _____

© 2006 Stephen Curran

7. Profit and Loss

Profit is the extra money made when something is sold for more than it was originally bought.
Loss is the money lost if something is sold for less than it was originally bought.

Example: A shopkeeper bought stock for **£3,000**. His other expenses totalled **£950** (rent, wages and electricity). If he sells the stock a month later for **£5,300**, what is his Gross Turnover and Net Profit?

Gross Turnover = £5,300
Net Profit = Gross Turnover − Expenses
= 5300 − (3000 + 950) = **£1,350**

Example: If the shopkeeper had the same expenses but sold the stock for only **£2,500**, what is his Gross Turnover and Net Loss?

Gross Turnover = £2,500
Net Loss = Expenses − Gross Turnover
= (3000 + 950) − 2500 = **£1,450**

Exercise 5: 6   Answer the following: Score ☐

1-10) Philip delivered leaflets in his local area for two four-day periods. He was paid at a rate of **£10** per thousand leaflets he delivered. Fill in the table and answer the questions.

	Day	Leaflets Delivered	Expenses	Profit £	Day	Leaflets Delivered	Expenses	Loss £
1)	Mon	4,000	£5.60	___	Mon	500	£7.60	___
2)	Tue	1,500	£5.00	___	Tue	1,000	£11.20	___
3)	Wed	3,500	£3.70	___	Wed	1,500	£17.80	___
4)	Thu	2,000	£7.20	___	Thu	500	£11.40	___
5)	Total	___	___	___	6) Total	___	___	

7) Total profit for period 1. ___   8) Total loss for period 2. ___
For the whole period worked, what was Philip's:
9) Gross income (before expenses)? ___
10) Net income (after expenses)? ___

8. Unit Costs

Some questions require the comparison of items and their cost to discover which gives the best value. This means the **Unit Cost** of each item has to be calculated (the cost per 100 grams of an item).

Example: At the supermarket there were various sizes of cans of soup. Which can gives the best value for money?

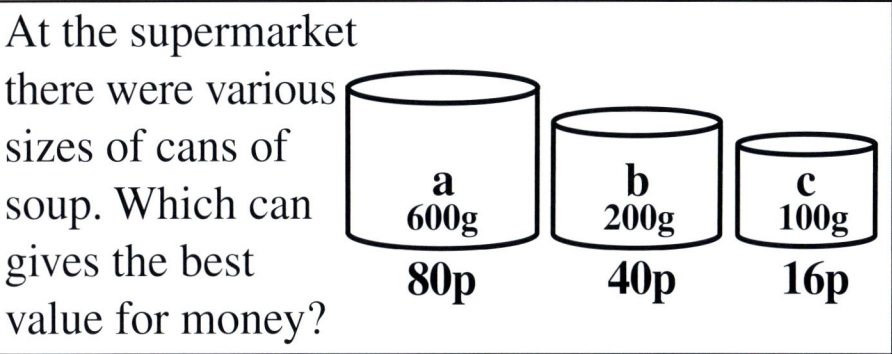

Find the price per 100g for each can by dividing the number of grams and the number of pence by the same number.

a) **600 ÷ 6 = 100**   b) **200 ÷ 2 = 100**   c) **100 ÷ 1 = 100**

   80 ÷ 6 = 13.3   **40 ÷ 2 = 20**   **16 ÷ 1 = 16**

   13.3p for **100g**   **20p** for **100g**   **16p** for **100g**

Can **a** is the best value because it offers 100g for the cheapest price.

Exercise 5: 7   Calculate the following: Score

1-10) A wholesaler sells different brands of bran flakes in various box sizes.

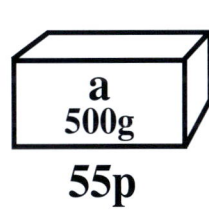 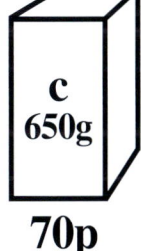 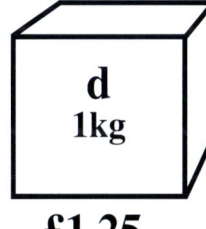 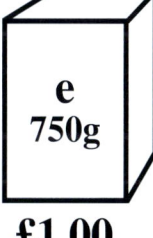

a 500g	b 250g	c 650g	d 1kg	e 750g
55p	40p	70p	£1.25	£1.00

What is the unit cost per 100g for each item?
Round to 2 d.p. where necessary.

1) **a** ___ p   2) **b** ___ p   3) **c** ___ p   4) **d** ___ p   5) **e** ___ p

Put the items in best value order:

6) 1st ___   7) 2nd ___   8) 3rd ___   9) 4th ___   10) 5th ___

9. More Money Problems

Exercise 5: 8 Calculate the following:

1) On a school trip a teacher buys **14** ice lollies at a cost of **£4.20** for about half his class of children. He then decides to buy the other **16** children the same ice lollies. What will the total cost be? £ _____

A supermarket sells cans of baked beans in two main sizes.

2) Which of the two sizes is better value? _____ g

3) How many of the better value cans can be bought for **£3**? _____ cans

500g — 40p   750g — 62p

4) Tim has a collection of comics. He has **three** worth **£2.75** each, **five** worth **£3.40** each and **ten** worth **£2.20** each. How much is his total collection worth?
£ _____

If **£5 = 950** Japanese yen what would be:

5) the exchange rate? **£1** = _____ yen
6) **665** yen in pounds? £_____   7) **£7.50** in yen? _____ yen

8) Patsy goes to the library to return **five** books, which are all overdue by one week. She gets **15p** change from a **£1** coin. The fine on each book was _____ p.

9) In a sale Melissa buys some stationery worth **£17.43**. She gets a **£1.36** discount and pays only £ _____.

10) Harpreet takes the bus from home to school and back again for **five** days each week. If each fare is **59p**, how much does she pay in fares in a **12** week term? £ _____

Chapter Six
MEASUREMENT
1. Metric Measures

These are SI Units. This is short for *Système International d'Unités* or the International System of Units. These units enable European countries to trade.

Kilo = 1000 : **Centi = $\frac{1}{100}$** : **Milli = $\frac{1}{1000}$**

Length or Distance

Measurements are made in: millimetres (mm), centimetres (cm), metres (m) and kilometres (km).

10 millimetres (mm)	= **1** centimetre (cm)
10 centimetres (cm)	= **1** decimetre (dm)
10 decimetres (dm)	= **1** metre (m)
1,000 millimetres (mm)	= **1** metre (m)
100 centimetres (cm)	= **1** metre (m)
1,000 metres (m)	= **1** kilometre (km)
100,000 centimetres (cm)	= **1** kilometre (km)

Weight (Mass)

Measurements are made in: grams (g), kilograms (kg) and tonnes (t).

1,000 milligrams (mg)	= **1** gram (g)
1,000 grams (g)	= **1** kilogram (kg)
1,000 kilograms (kg)	= **1** tonne (t)

Capacity (The space something takes up.)

Measurements are made in: millilitres (mℓ), centilitres (cℓ) and litres (ℓ).

10 millilitres (mℓ)	= **1** centilitre (cℓ)
1,000 millilitres (mℓ)	= **1** litre (ℓ)
100 centilitres (cℓ)	= **1** litre (ℓ)

Exercise 6: 1 Use the charts for conversion: Score

1) **1000g** = _____ **kg**   2) _____ **mm** = **1cm**

3) _____ **mℓ** = **1cℓ**   4) _____ **mm** = **1m**

5) **1t** = _____ **kg**   6) **1000mℓ** = _____ **ℓ**

7) **1ℓ** = _____ **cℓ**   8) **100mℓ** = _____ **cℓ**

9) _____ **cm** = **1m**   10) **1km** = _____ **m**

2. Metric Conversions

A quantity can be expressed in **Metric** form in many ways. All the amounts below are equal to each other.

metres	centimetres	millimetres	centimetres & millimetres
0.062m =	**6.2cm** =	**62mm** =	**6cm 2mm**

Conversions from one metric form to another can appear confusing. This **Four Step Conversion Method** can help.

Example: Change **5.3** metres to centimetres.

1. Find the conversion factor by asking this question.

   How many _smaller metric units_ are there in the _larger metric unit_ ?

   In this case - how many _centimetres_ are there in _a metre_ ?

   The conversion factor is **100** centimetres to a metre.

2. Breaking up or joining up? When we go from the original metric value to the new metric value, are we breaking up the amount into smaller units or are we joining it up to make larger units?

   Metres to centimetres means we are breaking up.

© 2006 Stephen Curran

3. More bits or less bits? If we break up the original metric value we end up with more bits. If we join it up we end up with less bits.

   Metres to centimetres means there will be more bits.

4. Move the decimal point right or left. The decimal point is moved left or right according to the number of zeros in the conversion factor. If there are more bits move the point to the right; if there are less bits move the point to the left.

   Move the decimal point 2 places to the right.

   5.3m is equivalent to 530cm.

Exercise 6: 2 Write in the equivalent amounts:

1) **7.5cm** = _____ mm or _____ cm and _____ mm

2) **8.2kg** = _____ g or _____ kg and _____ g

3) **9.1m** = _____ cm or _____ m and _____ cm

4) **3.68ℓ** = _____ cℓ or _____ mℓ

5) **643cℓ** = _____ ℓ or _____ ℓ and _____ cℓ

6) **1730m** = _____ km or _____ km and _____ m

7) **1243g** = _____ kg or _____ kg and _____ g

8) **37g** = _____ kg

9) **4.352m** = _____ cm and _____ mm

10) **6350mℓ** = _____ cℓ or _____ ℓ

Score

3. Metric Calculations

Calculations usually involve metric conversions. This must be done before any working out.

Example: The total mass of a box of oranges is **10kg**. Three customers buy **3.5kg**, **4½kg** and **1,200g** of oranges. If there are no oranges left, what was the net mass of the box in kilograms?

- Convert to kilograms (answer is to be in kg).
- Add the amounts.
- The **gross mass** of the box was **10kg**. To find the **net mass** (mass of the box after subtraction), subtract the mass of the oranges.

$$\begin{array}{r} 3.5 \\ 4.5 \\ 1.2+ \\ \hline 9.2 \end{array}$$

$$\begin{array}{r} {}^0 1{}^9 0 .{}^1 0 \\ 9.2 - \\ \hline 00.8 \end{array}$$

The net mass of the box was 0.8kg.

Exercise 6: 3   Calculate the following:

1) **7km + 8.53km + 700m** = _____ km

2) **6.87ℓ − 543mℓ** = _____ ℓ (Answer to 2 d.p.)

3) A piece of string is **3m 8cm** long. It is cut in half and then cut in half again. How long is each piece? (Convert and divide.) _____ cm

4) **8** boxes weigh **2½kg** each and **5** boxes weigh **900g** each. What is the total weight? (Convert, multiply, add.) _____ kg

5) **8025g ÷ 2.5** = _____ kg

6) A truck carrying cement has a gross mass of **8.15 tonnes**. If the cement being carried has a mass of **1,250kg** what is the net mass of the truck in tonnes? (Convert and subtract.) _____ tonnes

7) **435mℓ × 4** = _____ ℓ

8) Small cans of orangeade hold **160ml** and large cans hold **325ml**. Ranjeet drinks **seven** large and **three** small cans in a week. What was the total amount he drank? (Convert, multiply, add.) _____ ℓ (Answer to 2 d.p.)

9) Peter has **7m** of ribbon to wrap some gifts. He uses **70cm** each on two gifts. For a large gift he uses **2.3m**. He gives **90cm** of ribbon to his sister. How much ribbon does Peter have left? (Convert, multiply, add, subtract.) _____ m

10) A restaurant has **100ℓ** of bottled water. If each glass holds **300mℓ** of water, how many glasses can they fill? (Convert and divide.) _____ glasses

Score ☐

4. Imperial Measures

Imperial Units are still used and are measured as follows:

Weight - ounces, pounds, stones, centum weights and tons.

1 pound (lb) = **16** ounces (oz)
1 stone = **14** pounds (lbs)
1 cwt = **112** pounds (lbs)
2,240 lbs = **1** ton
20 cwt = **1** ton
160 stones = **1** ton

Length - inches, feet, yards, furlongs and miles.

1 foot (ft) = **12** inches
1 yard (yd) = **3** feet
1 furlong = **220** yards
8 furlongs = **1** mile (m)
1,760 yards = **1** mile (m)

Quantities

A dozen = **12**
A gross = **12** dozen (144)
A score = **20**

Capacity - pints, quarts and gallons.

1 pint = **20** fluid ounces
1 quart = **2** pints
1 gallon = **8** pints

5. Metric-Imperial Conversions

Learn these approximate (≈) conversions:

Length
- $2\frac{1}{2}$ cm ≈ 1 inch
- 30 cm ≈ 1 foot
- 1 m ≈ 1+ yards
- $1\frac{1}{2}$ km ≈ 1 mile
- 8 km ≈ 5 miles

Weight
- 30 g ≈ 1 ounce (oz)
- 1 kg ≈ 2+ pounds

+ here means 'a little bit more than'.

Capacity
- 1 metric tonne ≈ 1 imperial ton
- 1 litre ≈ 2 pints
- $4\frac{1}{2}$ litres ≈ 1 gallon

Exercise 6: 4   Estimate the following: Score

1) **3m** ≈ _____ yards   2) **10 pounds** ≈ _____ kg
3) **5 litres** ≈ _____ pints   4) **2 miles** ≈ _____ km
5) **3kg** ≈ _____ pounds   6) **4 inches** ≈ _____ cm
7) **24km** ≈ _____ miles   8) **6 pints** ≈ _____ litres
9) **5cm** ≈ _____ inches   10) **5 feet** ≈ _____ cm

Metric-imperial conversions can involve simple sums.

Example: A road sign says **90** miles to Norwich. Roughly how far is this in kilometres?

There are approximately **1.5** kilometres in one mile.
Multiply: 90 × 1.5 ≈ **135 kilometres**

Exercise 6: 5   Give approximate conversions: Score

1) Roughly how many yards are there in **50** metres?
   100yds   **51yds**   **150yds**   **200yds**   _____ yds

2) A girl weighs **110lbs**. What would this roughly be in kilograms?

   20kg   120kg   50kg   80kg   30kg   _____ kg

3) Mr Bain's swimming pool holds **45,000** litres of water. Roughly how many gallons is this?   _____ gallons

4) A man drives **40** miles to his place of work. Approximately how many kilometres would this be?

   200km   75km   66km   45km   28km   _____ km

5) A newborn baby weighs **3.5kg**. Roughly how many pounds is this?   _____ lbs

6) The world's heaviest man was alleged to be Jon Minnoch who weighed in at about **100** stones. What would his approximate weight be in kilograms?

   650kg   300kg   445kg   200kg   500kg   _____ kg

7) A sign on a low bridge states that only vehicles **3.5** metres tall can pass underneath. Can a lorry **13** feet high pass underneath. Yes or no?   _____

8) The length of a room is **20** feet. What is this in metres?

   12m   40m   4m   6m   8m   _____ m

9) Jenny is **5** feet **1** inch tall. What is her height roughly in metres?

   1.7m   2m   1.2m   1.5m   1.3m   _____ m

10) On Christmas day **9** inches of snow fell. Approximately how many centimetres is this?

    21cm   23cm   18cm   10cm   29cm   _____ cm

6. Estimating Measurements

An **Estimate** is a sensible guess or judgement. It is not based on a calculation that has been carried out.

15cm ≈	The length of a pencil.	250mℓ ≈	A mug of tea.
30cm ≈	An A4 piece of paper lengthways.	330mℓ ≈	A can of drink.
		1ℓ ≈	A bottle of squash.
1m ≈	The width of a single bed or an adult pace.	500g ≈	A can of beans.
		1kg ≈	A bag of sugar.

Estimation questions require an understanding of how measurements relate to everyday things.

Example: A coffee pot holds enough for **five** mugs of coffee. Which is the most likely volume?

~~3 litres~~   0.7 litres   ~~200mℓ~~   ~~7 litres~~   1.3 litres
too big   too small   too big

1. Rule out amounts that are obviously too big or small.
2. Relate amounts to something similar on the chart.
5 mugs will be about 1.3 litres.

Exercise 6: 6   Estimate the following: Score

1) A medium-sized teapot holds enough for four cups of tea. Which volume is most likely to be true?

   2.5ℓ   0.4ℓ   300mℓ   4ℓ   800mℓ   _____

2) Fifteen children at a birthday party each drink one glass of lemonade. How much did they drink in total?

   4ℓ   600mℓ   8ℓ   1,200mℓ   2ℓ   _____

3) What is the approximate weight of three boxes of cereal?
7kg   1.5kg   9kg   100g   300g _____

4) What would ten telephone directories roughly weigh?
200kg   25kg   2kg   70g   120kg _____

5) A boy of 10 years paces out the length of his bedroom to find out how big it is. If he measures it as 10 paces, what is the likely distance in feet?
14ft   10ft   18ft   20ft   30ft _____ ft

6) A family of four packs a picnic bag. It contains two large bottles of lemonade, a flask of tea, a round of sandwiches and four apples. What is the likely weight?
15kg   100g   5kg   500g   20g _____

7) A lorry carrying **100** sacks of cabbages comes to a bridge displaying a sign *Maximum Weight 9.5 tonnes*. The lorry weighs **5** tonnes and the weight of each sack is **50kg**. Is it safe for the lorry to cross? Yes or no? _____

8) What would a pile of ten CDs with cases approximately weigh? **10kg   60g   1kg   5kg   100g** _____

9) Which container has a capacity of about **5** litres?
teacup   bottle   teapot   bucket   bath _____

10) Dr Fuller's car is **4** metres long. This is the average length of all **4** cars at the surgery. A parking bay has to be marked out along the roadside. If an extra **1.5m** gap is allowed for each car to drive into the space, how long does the bay have to be for all the cars to be parked?
27m   17m   20m   24m   30m _____ m

7. Reading Metric Scales

Decimals are used when reading off **Scales**. Measuring jugs, rulers and weight scales all make use of decimal scales.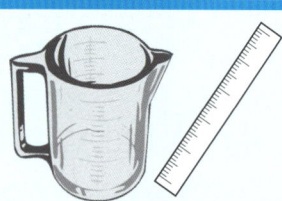

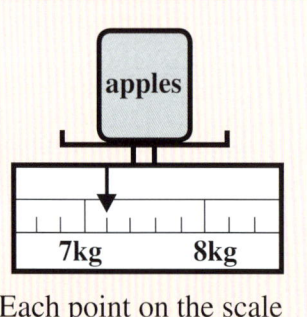

Each point on the scale represents **200g** or **0.2kg**.

Example:

The arrow indicates how much a sack of apples weighs. If another **900g** of apples are added, what will the total weight be?

1. Convert **900g** into kg = **0.9kg**
2. Add 0.9kg + 7.2kg = **8.1kg**

Exercise 6: 7   Calculate the following: Score

Three glass beakers are filled with measures of water.

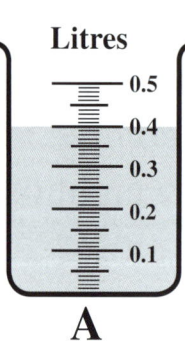 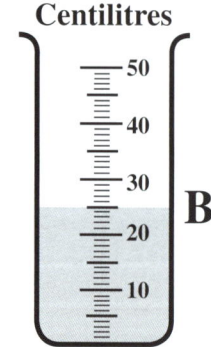 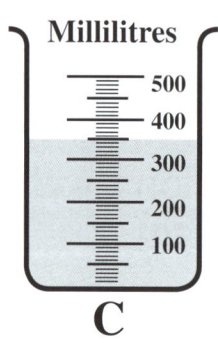

Convert the following measures into the required units:

1) **A** is ____ cl 2) **B** is ____ ml 3) **C** is ____ l 4) **B** is ____ l

5) Add **A** and **B**.   6) Subtract **B** from **C**.   7) Add **A** and **C**.
   ____ millilitres   ____ litres   ____ centilitres

8) Oranges are weighed on a scale:

a) What does each individual orange weigh?
   ____ g

b) Give the weight in kg if another **12** oranges are added. ____ kg

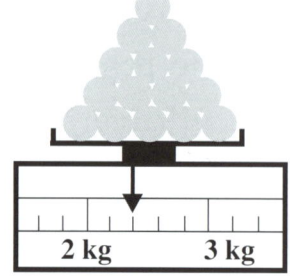

9) Convert the distance indicated above into metres. _____ m

10) If **1,450mm** were added to this measurement what would the new distance be in centimetres? _____ cm

8. Temperature

Temperature is the measurement of how hot or cold something is. It is most commonly used to describe how hot or cold the air is in a particular place.

Temperature is measured using a thermometer in degrees Celsius (°C). A thermometer contains the liquid ethanol, which rises and falls depending on the temperature.

Water boils at **100°C** and it freezes at **0°C**.

Temperature measurements can be either **Positive** or **Negative**, in the same way as on this number line:

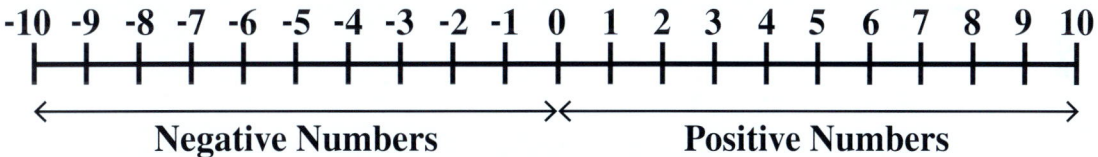

Negative numbers are used to show very cold temperatures below **0°C** (**zero**).

Example: What temperature is shown on the thermometer?

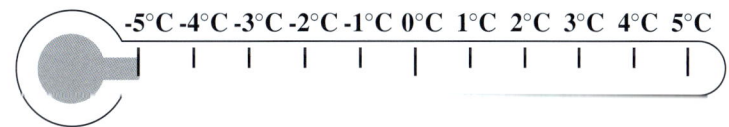

The liquid level in the thermometer rests at **-5°C** meaning that is the temperature.

Answer: **-5°C**

Exercise 6: 8

What temperature is shown on the thermometer?

1) 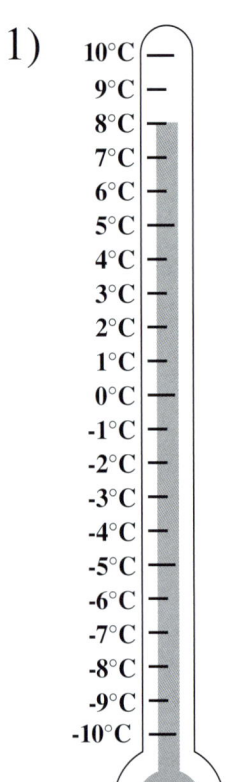   2) 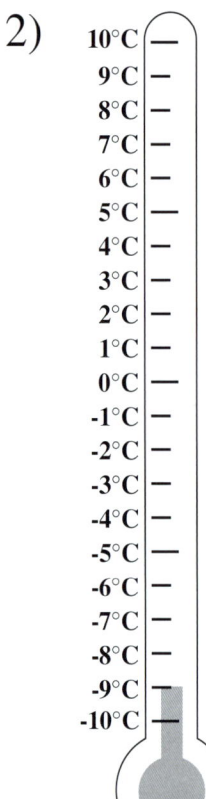   3) 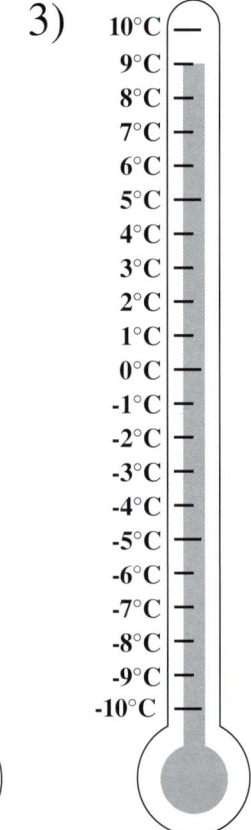   4)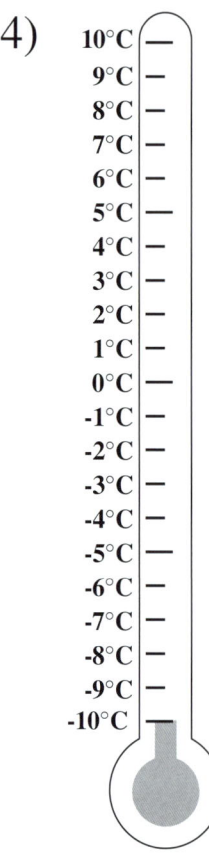

5) 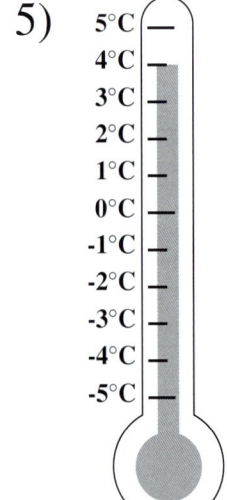   6) 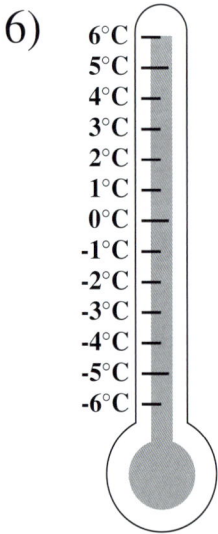   7) 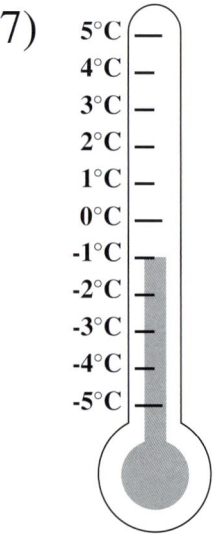   8)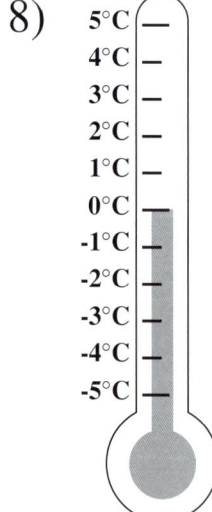

9) 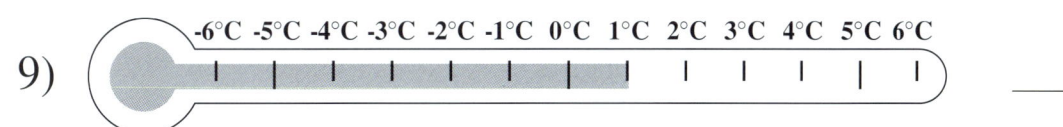 _____

10) 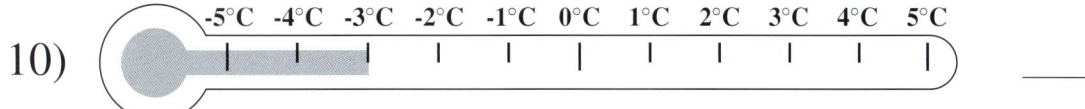 _____

Example: What is the difference in temperature between **-1°C** and **3°C**?

Use a number line to count the gaps between **-1°C** and **3°C**.

Do not subtract one number from the other, e.g. **3 – 1 = 2**, as this is incorrect.

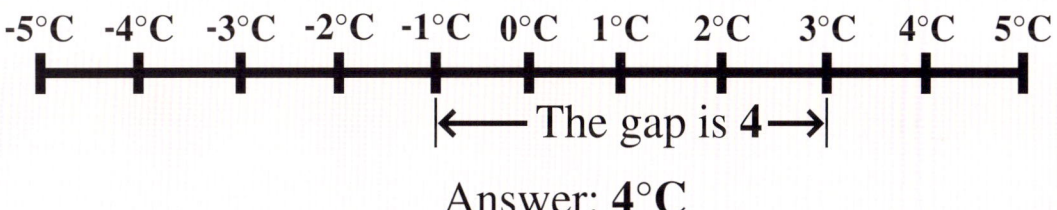

Answer: **4°C**

Exercise 6: 9   Answer the following:

1) The starting temperature was **-4°C**. The temperature fell by **20°C**. What is the new temperature? _____

2) What is the difference in temperature between **-15°C** and **15°C**? _____

3) The temperature at midday was **-9°C**. By nightfall the temperature had fallen by **18°C**. What was the temperature overnight? _____

4) What is the difference in temperature between **-3°C** and **-20°C**? ____

5) The temperature started at **-14°C**. It rose by **17°C**. What was the new temperature? ____

6) What is the difference in temperature between **-12°C** and **11°C**? ____

7) The temperature in the city fell by **9°C** overnight. It started at **8°C**. What was the new temperature? ____

8) What is the difference in temperature between **9°C** and **-11°C**? ____

9) Overnight the temperature was **-13°C**. During the morning it rose by **12°C**. What was the new temperature? ____

10) What is the difference in temperature between **-3°C** and **-1°C**? ____

9. Measurement Problems

Exercise 6: 10 Calculate the following. Use the conversion charts in this chapter if necessary.

1) Convert this recipe for fruit salad from imperial to metric units (to the nearest 5g).

Type of Fruit	Imperial	Metric
a) Apple	7oz	____ g
b) Orange	12oz	____ g
c) Banana	10oz	____ g

2) Kisham is **4** feet **11** inches tall. Which is closest to his height in metres?

   1.4m   1.7m   1.6m   1.5m   1.8m _____

3) A grocer sells the following fruit in one morning:

   3kg of grapefruit at **£1.10** per kg.
   5kg of apples at **80p** per kg.
   4kg of grapes at **£1.30** per kg.
   9kg of bananas at **50p** per kg.

   What would his total takings be for the morning?
   £ _____

4) $1\frac{1}{2}$**m** of cloth costs **£1.80**. Find the cost of:

   a) **6.5m**. £ _____   b) **9m**. £ _____   c) $3\frac{1}{2}$**m**. £ _____

5) **15** metres of carpet cost **£375**. How much will **25** metres cost? £ _____

6) **5** litres of orange squash cost **£3.20**. How much will **8** litres cost? £ _____

7) Write these amounts in metres:

   a) **9m 25cm** _____ m   b) **35mm** _____ m

8) Write the following as decimals:

   a) $11\frac{3}{10}$**m** _____ m   b) $2\frac{7}{20}$**m** _____ m   c) $4\frac{3}{5}$**m** _____ m

9) Underline the weights which are greater than $\frac{1}{2}$**kg**.

   510g   **465g**   **0.45kg**   **0.501kg**   **550g**

10) Write these weights in tonnes and kilograms:

    a) **8.7t** ____ t ____ kg   b) $5\frac{4}{5}$**t** ____ t ____ kg

Score

Chapter Seven
AVERAGES
1. Mode, Median and Range

Mode = Most common value

Median = Middle value

Range = Distance between the smallest and the biggest

Mode, **Median** and **Range** can be found from a series of numbers given in a mixed up order.

Example:

Find the mode, median and range of these numbers.
9, 7, 3, 4, 4, 3, 1, 6, 4

1. Rearrange them in size order.

   1, 3, 3, 4, 4, 4, 6, 7, 9

2. Count the numbers to check all of them have been used. (There are 9 numbers.)

3. Mode - the most common value.

   1, 3, 3, **4, 4, 4**, 6, 7, 9

   The mode is 4 - it occurs 3 times.

4. Median - the middle value.

$$1, \quad 3, \quad 3, \quad 4, \quad \mathbf{4}, \quad 4, \quad 6, \quad 7, \quad 9$$

$\leftarrow$ Four numbers this side. $\uparrow$ Four numbers this side. $\rightarrow$

Median = 4

5. Range - the distance from the smallest to the biggest.

$$\mathbf{1}, \quad 3, \quad 3, \quad 4, \quad 4, \quad 4, \quad 6, \quad 7, \quad \mathbf{9}$$

The smallest is **1** and the biggest is **9**.

Subtract **9 − 1 = 8**   **The range is 8.**

Exercise 7: 1   Calculate the mode, median or range:

4, 12, 6, 14, 15, 12, 11

1) Mode: _____   2) Median: _____   3) Range: _____

1, 3, 13, 10, 25, 3, 14, 7

4) Mode: _____   5) Median: _____

6) Range: _____   (As there are 8 numbers, the median is halfway between the 4th and the 5th digit - a decimal value.)

7-8) The table below shows children's attendance at a youth club over **10** weeks.

Week	1	2	3	4	5	6	7	8	9	10
Attendance	27	25	31	30	28	27	29	26	27	30

Find the:

7) Mode. _____   8) Median. _____

9-10) Sahiba played a computer game **9** times. Her scores were:

21, **40**, **10**, **16**, **5**, **17**, **5**, **3**, **0**

Find the:

9) Median. _____ 10) Range. _____

Score

2. The 'Mean' or Average

When asked to give an **Average** it refers to the **'Mean'**.

Mean = Total of all the items ÷ Number of items

a. Amount to 'Mean'

If separate amounts are given the mean can be found.

Example: Find the average of **5**, **7**, **8**, **4**, **4**, **3**, **1**, **6** and **7**.

1. Add the numbers. $5 + 7 + 8 + 4 + 4 + 3 + 1 + 6 + 7 = 45$

2. Divide by the number of items. $\dfrac{45}{9}$ = **The mean is 5.**

Exercise 7: 2a   Calculate the following:

1) What is the average of **21**, **17** and **16**? _____

2) Find the average of **3.5**, **5.0** and **0.5**. _____

3) What is the mean of **9**, **12**, **14** and **13**? _____

78   © 2006 Stephen Curran

4) A man's lunches for a week cost **£1.15**, **75p**, **85p**, **£1.45**, **£1.25** and **55p**. What is the average cost?
£ _____

5) The temperatures during a week's holiday were:

S	M	T	W	Th	F	S
23	28	21	24	25	27	25

Find the mean temperature correct to one decimal place.
_____ °C

b. 'Mean' to Total

If the 'mean' is given, the total can be found.

Example: The average weight of three boys was **37.5kg**. What was their total weight?

1. The weight of the three boys is different, but an average has already been calculated (**37.5kg**).

2. Multiply the average by the number of boys (×3).
   37.5 × 3 = 112.5kg

Total = Mean × Number of items

Exercise 7: 2b   Calculate the following:

6) The average cost of **4** articles was **£1.25**. What was the total cost? £ _____

7) The mean height of **5** girls was **145cm**. Give their total height in metres. _____ m

c. 'Mean' to Amount

> If the 'mean' is given, an amount can be found.

Example: Gary's birthday is on Saturday. He receives birthday cards through the week (an average of **6** a day over the week). How many did he receive on Thursday?

1. Find the total - multiply the mean by the number of days.
   $6 \times 5 = 30$

2. Add the given amounts.
   $5 + 7 + 1 + 8 = 21$

3. Subtract the given amounts from the total.
   $30 - 21 = 9$

Day	Number of cards
Mon	5
Tue	7
Wed	1
Thurs	?
Fri	8

The mean is **6**.

He received 9 cards on Thursday.

Exercise 7: 2c Score

Milkshake	No. of pupils
Vanilla	?
Strawberry	23
Banana	14
Raspberry	6

The mean is **15**.

8) Year 6 conducted a survey on their favourite flavour of milkshake.

How many children liked vanilla? _____

9) The average spending of four girls was **£5.50**. Three of the girls spent **£3.20**, **£6.25** and **£5.10**. How much did the fourth girl spend? £ _____

10) The average (mean) age of seven children is **10** years. The average (mean) age of six of the children is **9** years. How old is the seventh child? _____ years

3. More Average Problems

Exercise 7: 3 Calculate the following: Score

These are the numbers of letters received by a small business each day for a week.

    23   **13**   **57**   **21**   **21**

Find the following average values: 1) Mean. _____

2) Mode. _____   3) Median. _____   4) Range. _____

5) The mean cost of five books is **£3.50**. What is the total cost? £ _____

6) Another book is added which costs **£6.50**. What is the new mean cost? £ _____

Sanesh does a survey on how much tea his father drinks in one week. His father keeps a record, but forgets to write down how many cups he drank on Wednesday. He believes he drinks about **6** cups a day (treat this as the mean).

Day	Mon	Tues	Wed	Thurs	Fri	Sat	Sun
Cups of Tea	6	7	?	5	6	4	10

7) How many cups were drunk on Wednesday? _____ cups

8) What is the median value? _____ cups

9) What is the range? _____

10) In the following week he restricts his tea drinking to a total of **21** cups. What is the new mean amount for that week? _____ cups

Chapter Eight
BASES
1. What is a Base?

A **Base** is a pattern of counting. The name of the base comes from the main counting unit.
The **Tens Number System** (Decimal System) or **Denary** is the basis for most counting. An abacus can be used.

Example: **4,321** shown as base **10**.

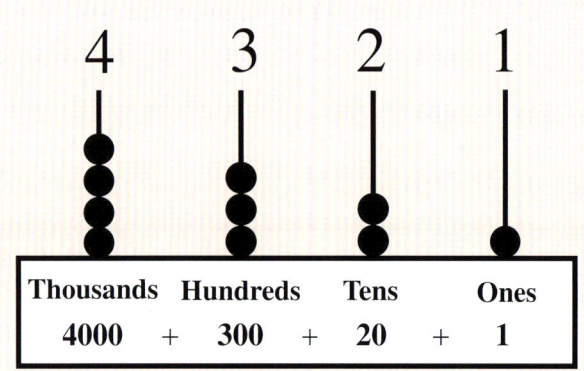

The number as base **10** is 4321_{10}

Counting in groups of **ten** (from **0** up to **9** in each column).

Four groups of **1000**
Three groups of **100**
Two groups of **10**
1 one

The base is shown at the foot of the number.

2. Base 2 (Binary)

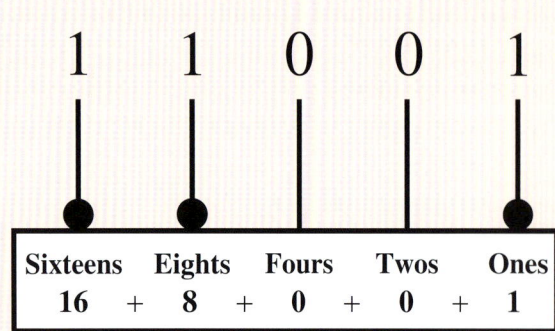

$25_{10} = 11001_2$

Base **2** is termed **Binary**. Counting in groups of **two** (up to **1** in each column).
Example:
Convert 25_{10} to base **2**.

One group of **16**
One group of **8**
1 one

Exercise 8: 1 Convert from base **10** to base **2**:

Score

1) 10_{10} = ____$_2$

Eights	Fours	Twos	Ones

2) 17_{10} = ____$_2$

Sixteens	Eights	Fours	Twos	Ones

3) 7_{10} = ____$_2$ 4) 12_{10} = ____$_2$ 5) 31_{10} = ____$_2$

Convert from base **2** to base **10**:

6)
Eights	Fours	Twos	Ones
1	1	1	1_2

= ____$_{10}$ 7) 101_2 = ____$_{10}$

8) 110_2 = ____$_{10}$ 9) 1011_2 = ____$_{10}$ 10) 11101_2 = ____$_{10}$

a. Adding and Subtracting in Base 2

It follows the normal pattern except each column can only show digits **0** or **1**.

Examples:

Add $111_2 + 110_2$

$$\begin{array}{r} 1\,1\,1_2 \\ 1\,1\,0_2 + \\ \hline 1\,1\,0\,1_2 \\ {}_{1\ \ 1} \end{array}$$

Base 10
$$\begin{array}{r} 7 \\ 6 + \\ \hline 13 \end{array}$$

$1 + 0 = 1$
Place **1** in column 1.
$1 + 1 = 2$
Place **0** in column 2, carry **1**.
$1 + 1 + 1 = 3$
Place **1** in column 3, carry **1**.
Place **1** in column 4.

Subtract $1001_2 - 110_2$

$$\begin{array}{r} {}^0\cancel{1}{}^{+2}0\,{}^{+2}0\,1_2 \\ {}^2\cancel{1}\,1\,0_2 - \\ \hline 0\,0\,1\,1_2 \end{array}$$

Base 10
$$\begin{array}{r} 9 \\ 6 - \\ \hline 3 \end{array}$$

$1 - 0 = 1$
Place **1** in column 1.
Borrow **2**; $2 - 1 = 1$
Place **1** in column 2, pay back **1**.
Borrow **2**; $2 - 2 = 0$
Place **0** in column 3.
Place **0** in column 4.

© 2006 Stephen Curran

Exercise 8: 2 Calculate the following:

1) 1101_2
   $101_2 +$
   ———

2) 1001_2
   $101_2 +$
   ———

3) 1010_2
   $10_2 -$
   ———

4) 11011_2
   $1101_2 -$
   ———

5) 1001_2
   $111_2 +$
   ———

6) 1111_2
   $100_2 +$
   ———

7) 1101_2
   $11_2 -$
   ———

8) 10010_2
   $1001_2 -$
   ———

9) 1101_2
   $1011_2 +$
   ———

10) 10101_2
    $1010_2 -$
    ———

Score

3. Counting in Other Bases

Methods of counting can be worked out through indices.

Power of 4	Power of 3	Power of 2	Base No.	Ones	Base
$2^4 = 16s$ $(2 \times 2 \times 2 \times 2)$	$2^3 = 8s$ $(2 \times 2 \times 2)$	$2^2 = 4s$ (2×2)	2s	1s	**2** (Binary)
81s	27s	9s	3s	1s	**3** (Ternary)
256s	64s	16s	4s	1s	**4**
625s	125s	25s	5s	1s	**5**
1296s	216s	36s	6s	1s	**6**
2401s	343s	49s	7s	1s	**7**
4096s	512s	64s	8s	1s	**8** (Octal)
6561s	729s	81s	9s	1s	**9**

Base **10** = **Denary/Decimal** system

Base **12** = **Duodecimal** system

Base **16** = **Hexadecimal** system (Used mainly by computers.)

Convert 25_{10} to base 3.	Convert 25_{10} to base 5.
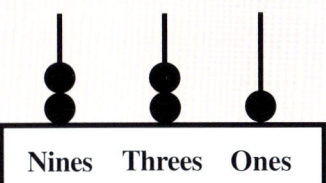	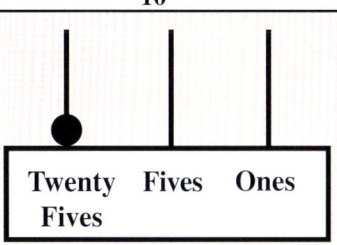
Base 3 is called **Ternary**. Counting in groups of **three** (up to **2** in each column).	Base **5** Counting in groups of **five** (up to **4** in each column).
$25_{10} = 221_3$	$25_{10} = 100_5$
Two groups of 9 Two groups of 3 1 One	One group of 25

Exercise 8: 3 Convert the following: Score ☐

Convert from base 10 to base 3.

1) $87_{10} = $ _____$_3$

Eighty Ones	Twenty Sevens	Nines	Threes	Ones

2) $58_{10} = $ _____$_3$

Twenty Sevens	Nines	Threes	Ones

Convert from base 3 to base 10.

3)
Nines	Threes	Ones
2	1	2_3
= _____$_{10}$

4) $2110_3 = $ _____$_{10}$

5) $12120_3 = $ _____$_{10}$

Convert from base 10 to base 5.

6) $79_{10} = $ _____$_5$

Twenty Fives	Fives	Ones

7) $269_{10} = $ _____$_5$

One hundred & twenty Fives	Twenty Fives	Fives	Ones

Convert from base 5 to base 10.

8) $241_5 = $ _____$_{10}$ 9) $404_5 = $ _____$_{10}$ 10) $233_5 = $ _____$_{10}$

a. Adding and Subtracting in Base 3 and 5

| Base **3** columns can only show digits **0**, **1** and **2**. | Base **5** columns can only show digits **0**, **1**, **2**, **3** and **4**. |

Example: Add $112_3 + 12_3$

$$\begin{array}{r} 112_3 \\ 12_3\, + \\ \hline 201_3 \\ {}^{1\ 1} \end{array} \qquad \begin{array}{|r|} \hline \text{Base 10} \\ 14 \\ 5\, + \\ \hline 19 \\ \hline \end{array}$$

$2 + 2 = 4$
Place **1** in column 1, carry **1**.
$1 + 1 + 1 = 3$
Place **0** in column 2, carry **1**.
$1 + 1 = 2$
Place **2** in column 3.

Example: Subtract $221_5 - 34_5$

$$\begin{array}{r} {}^{+5\ +5} \\ \cancel{2}^{12}\cancel{2} 1_5 \\ 34_5\, - \\ \hline 132_5 \end{array} \qquad \begin{array}{|r|} \hline \text{Base 10} \\ 61 \\ 19\, - \\ \hline 42 \\ \hline \end{array}$$

Borrow **5**; $6 - 4 = 2$
Place **2** in column 1.
Borrow **5**; $6 - 3 = 3$
Place **3** in column 2.
$1 - 0 = 1$
Place **1** in column 3.

Exercise 8: 4   Calculate the following: Score

1) $\begin{array}{r} 2212_3 \\ 202_3\, + \\ \hline \end{array}$

2) $\begin{array}{r} 1021_3 \\ 122_3\, - \\ \hline \end{array}$

3) $\begin{array}{r} 3444_5 \\ 344_5\, + \\ \hline \end{array}$

4) $\begin{array}{r} 2442_5 \\ 1344_5\, - \\ \hline \end{array}$

5) $\begin{array}{r} 2112_3 \\ 220_3\, + \\ \hline \end{array}$

6) $\begin{array}{r} 2022_3 \\ 222_3\, - \\ \hline \end{array}$

7) $\begin{array}{r} 3341_5 \\ 44_5\, + \\ \hline \end{array}$

8) $\begin{array}{r} 2404_5 \\ 1040_5\, - \\ \hline \end{array}$

Which base has been used in these sums?

9) $\begin{array}{r} 3231 \\ 1021\, + \\ \hline 10312 \end{array}$ Base ____

10) $\begin{array}{r} 1001 \\ 11\, - \\ \hline 110 \end{array}$ Base ____

4. Multiplying Bases

a. Short Multiplication

(i) Short Multiplication in Base 4

It follows the normal pattern of multiplication except in base **4** each column can only show digits **0** to **3**.

Example: Multiply $323_4 \times 3$

$$323_4$$
$$\underline{3 \times}$$
$$\underline{2301_4}$$
$$22$$

$3 \times 3 = 9$
Carry **2** groups of **4** with **1** left over.
$3 \times 2 = 6 + 2 = 8$
Carry **2** groups of **4** with **0** left over.
$3 \times 3 = 9 + 2 = 11$
Carry **2** groups of **4** with **3** left over.
Place **2** in column 4.

Base 10
$$59$$
$$\underline{3 \times}$$
$$\underline{177}$$

Answer: In base 4 it is 2301_4 and in base 10 it is 177_{10}

Exercise 8: 5a Calculate the following:

1) 401_5
   $3 \times$

2) 222_3
   $2 \times$

3) 505_8
   $7 \times$

4) 322_6
   $5 \times$

5) 85_9
   $6 \times$

b. Long Multiplication

(ii) Long Multiplication in Base 6

In base **6** each column can only show digits **0** to **5**.

Example: Multiply $145_6 \times 43_6$

$$145_6$$
$$43_6 \times$$
—
$$523_6$$
$$_{2\ 2}$$

Line One
$3 \times 5 = 15$
Carry **2** groups of **6** with **3** left over.
$3 \times 4 = 12 + 2 = 14$
Carry **2** groups of **6** with **2** left over.
$3 \times 1 = 3 + 2 = 5$
Place **5** in column 3.

$$145_6$$
$$43_6 \times$$
—
$$523_6$$
- - - - -
$$11120_6$$
$$_{1\ 3\ 3}$$
$$12043_6$$
$$_1$$

Base 10
$$65$$
$$27 \times$$
—
$$1755$$

Line Two
Zero in.
$4 \times 5 = 20$
Carry **3** groups of **6** with **2** left over.
$4 \times 4 = 16 + 3 = 19$
Carry **3** groups of **6** with **1** left over.
$4 \times 1 = 4 + 3 = 7$
Carry **1** group of **6** with **1** left over.
Place **1** in column 5.
Line Three - Add in base **6**.

Answer: In base 6 it is 12043_6 and in base 10 it is 1755_{10}

Exercise 8: 5b Multiply the following:

6) $$1010_2$$
$$11_2 \times$$

7) $$312_4$$
$$32_4 \times$$

8) $$64_7$$
$$52_7 \times$$

9) $$431_5$$
$$23_5 \times$$

10) $$136_8$$
$$47_8 \times$$

Score

5. Dividing Bases
a. Short Division in Base 7 and 8

It follows the normal pattern of division except in base **7** each column can only show digits **0** to **6**, and in base **8** each column can only show digits **0** to **7**.

Example: Divide $132_7 \div 4$

Base 7

$$4 \overline{) 1\,3^{10}2^{16}_{7}} = 0\,2\,4_7$$

Base 7
$1 \div 4$ will not divide.
Add **1** group of remainder **7** to **3** to make **10**.
$10 \div 4 = 2$ with **2** groups of **7** remainder.
Add **2** groups of remainder **7** to **2** to make **16**.
$16 \div 4 = 4$

Base 10

$$4 \overline{) 7\,{}^3 2_{10}} = 1\,8_{10}$$

Base 10
The same sum can be written in base **10**.
$7 \div 4 = 1$ with **3** groups of **10** remainder.
Add **3** groups of remainder **10** to **2** to make **32**.
$32 \div 4 = 8$

Answer: In base 7 it is 24_7 and in base 10 it is 18_{10}

Example: Divide $2651_8 \div 7$

Base 8

$$7 \overline{) 2\,6^{22}5^{13}1^{49}_{8}} = 0\,3\,1\,7_8$$

Base 8
$2 \div 7$ will not divide.
Add **2** groups of remainder **8** to **6** to make **22**.
$22 \div 7 = 3$ with **1** group of **8** remainder.
Add **1** group of remainder **8** to **5** to make **13**.
$13 \div 7 = 1$ with **6** groups of **8** remainder.
Add **6** groups of remainder **8** to **1** to make **49**.
$49 \div 7 = 7$

Base 10

$$7 \overline{) 1\,4^{14}4^{4}9_{10}} = 0\,2\,0\,7_{10}$$

Base 10
The same sum can be written in base **10**.
$1 \div 7 = 0$ with a remainder of **1** group of **10**.
Add **1** group of remainder **10** to **4** to make **14**.
$14 \div 7 = 2$
$4 \div 7 = 0$ with a remainder of **4** groups of **10**.
Add **4** groups of remainder **10** to **1** to make **49**.
$49 \div 7 = 7$

Answer: In base 8 it is 317_8 and in base 10 it is 207_{10}

Exercise 8: 6 Divide the following:

1) $2\overline{)1210}_3$ 2) $2\overline{)324}_6$ 3) $2\overline{)10102}_3$

4) $6\overline{)3162}_8$ 5) $3\overline{)2434}_5$ 6) $3\overline{)10233}_4$

7) $8\overline{)2752}_{10}$ 8) $5\overline{)6451}_7$ 9) $3\overline{)2753}_9$

10) $3\overline{)10323}_4$

Score

6. Mixed Exercises

Exercise 8: 7 Calculate the following:

Score

Convert from base **10** to base **7**:

1) 62_{10} = _____$_7$

Convert from base **9** to base **10**:

2) 242_9 = _____$_{10}$

3) 1202_4
   $123_4 +$
   _____

4) 3543_6
   $1215_6 +$
   _____

5) 6213_7
   $2342_7 -$
   _____

6) 5146_8
   $4307_8 -$
   _____

7) a) 432_5
      $3 \times$
      _____

   b) 132_4
      $2 \times$
      _____

8) 526_7
   $43_7 \times$
   _____
   - - - - - - - - - - -
   _____

9) $2\overline{)10201}_3$

10) $5\overline{)15384}_9$

Answers

11+ Maths Year 5-7 Workbook 2

Chapter Four
Fractions
Exercise 4: 1
1) $3/4$ 2) $4/9$
3) $8/3$ 4) $9/10$
5) $5/7$ 6) $6 \div 7$
7) $4 \div 5$ 8) $2 \div 9$
9) $1 \div 6$ 10) $2 \div 5$

Exercise 4: 2
1) $5/5$ 2) $10/10$
3) $6/6$ 4) $7/7$
5) $9/9$ 6) $16/16$
7) $8/8$ 8) $12/12$
9) 1   10) 1

Exercise 4: 3
1) $2/3$ 2) $5/6$
3) $3/5$ 4) $7/10$
5) $1/4$ 6) $3/10$
7) $1/6$ 8) $3/8$
9) $7/8$ 10) $2/5$

Exercise 4: 4
1) $1/6$ 2) $3/8$
3) $2/5$ 4) $3/10$
5) $1/3$ 6) $5/12$
7) $3/20$ 8) $1/4$
9) $1/6$ 10) $16/33$

Exercise 4: 5
1) $3/4$ 2) $4/10$
3) $2/3$ 4) $10/16$
5) $6/10$ 6) $8/12$
7) $14/16$ 8) $1/3$
9) $1/2$ 10) $1/5$

Exercise 4: 6
1) 4   2) 5
3) 5   4) 6
5) 6   6) 4
7) 12   8) 3
9) 9   10) 25

Exercise 4: 7
1) $1/3$ 2) $2/3$ 3) $1/6$
4) $5/6$ 5) $1/4$ 6) $1/3$
7) $7/9$ 8) $5/8$ 9) $6/7$
10) $4/5$

Exercise 4: 8
1) $1/4$ 2) $1/3$ 3) $1/4$
4) $1/4$ 5) $1/2$ 6) $1/3$
7) $2/5$ 8) $2/5$ 9) $1/3$
10) $1/5$

Exercise 4: 9
1) $6/9$ 2) $6/12$ 3) $4/5$
4) $15/24$ 5) $6/18$ 6) $11/15$
7) $15/20$ 8) $18/30$ 9) $5/6$
10) $35/40$

Exercise 4: 10a
1) Proper   2) Improper
3) Improper 4) Proper
5) Improper

Exercise 4: 10b
6) $6/2$ 7) $12/6$ 8) $35/7$
9) $63/9$ 10) $72/12$

Exercise 4: 11
Simplify the fractions if possible.
1) $13/8$ 2) $10/6 = 5/3$
3) $8/5$ 4) $15/8$
5) $26/10 = 13/5$ 6) $41/8$
7) $69/10$ 8) $44/12 = 11/3$
9) $44/6 = 22/3$ 10) $26/3$

Exercise 4: 12
1) $2\,3/8$ 2) $1\,1/3$
3) $2\,5/6$ 4) $3\,7/10$
5) $2\,7/12$ 6) $3\,1/6$
7) $1\,4/5$ 8) $2\,2/3$
9) $6\,5/7$ 10) $3\,7/9$

Exercise 4: 13
1) $5/2$ 2) $23/4$
3) $29/9$ 4) $14/3$
5) $31/7$ 6) $11/6$
7) $77/8$ 8) $34/5$
9) $95/9$ 10) $87/10$

Exercise 4: 14
1) $1\,1/3$ 2) $2\,1/2$
3) $1\,1/6$ 4) $4\,1/4$
5) $2\,2/7$ 6) 4
7) $3\,1/8$ 8) $2\,3/10$
9) $6\,1/3$ 10) $3\,4/9$

Exercise 4: 15
1) 18   2) 12
3) 18   4) 9
5) 20   6) 35
7) 48   8) 60
9) 12   10) 20

Exercise 4: 16a
1) $9/11$ 2) $3/4$
3) $11/13$ 4) $1\,1/2$
5) $1\,4/5$

Exercise 4: 16b
6) $23/30$ 7) $2/3$
8) $8/9$ 9) $2\,1/4$
10) $1\,31/42$

Exercise 4: 17
1) $6\,1/6$ 2) $10\,1/12$
3) $7\,3/20$ 4) $17\,5/8$
5) $5\,11/30$ 6) $4\,4/9$
7) $4\,9/20$ 8) $3\,11/16$
9) $13\,18/35$ 10) $11\,19/40$

Exercise 4: 18a
1) $2/11$ 2) $1/2$
3) $6/13$ 4) $1/2$
5) $1/5$

Exercise 4: 18b
6) $7/30$ 7) $1/4$
8) $1/18$ 9) $8/21$
10) $11/56$

11+ Maths
Year 5-7 Workbook 2

Answers

Exercise 4: 19a
1) $4^1/_{10}$ 2) $3^1/_8$
3) $2^{11}/_{40}$ 4) $3^1/_6$
5) $2^1/_4$ 6) $4^3/_8$

Exercise 4: 19b
7) $7^{13}/_{18}$ 8) $^5/_{12}$
9) $5^{17}/_{36}$ 10) $74^5/_8$

Exercise 4: 20
1) $^5/_{24}$ 2) $^{17}/_{20}$
3) $2^{17}/_{20}$ 4) $1^1/_3$
5) $3^7/_{18}$ 6) $2^3/_4$
7) $^{17}/_{20}$ 8) $^7/_{24}$
9) $2^1/_{12}$ 10) $1^5/_{16}$

Exercise 4: 21a
1) $^3/_{20}$ 2) $^{10}/_{77}$
3) $^8/_{45}$

Exercise 4: 21b
4) $^1/_2$ 5) $^1/_4$
6) $^1/_4$ 7) $^1/_{12}$
8) $^2/_3$ 9) $^4/_7$
10) $^8/_{35}$

Exercise 4: 22
1) $4^1/_3$ 2) $^{13}/_{16}$
3) $10^1/_2$ 4) 6
5) $^2/_5$ 6) 21
7) $2^1/_{16}$ 8) 2
9) $^{32}/_{33}$ 10) $^1/_5$

Exercise 4: 23
1) $1^1/_2$ 2) $1^1/_4$
3) $^1/_2$ 4) 1
5) 1 6) $^2/_3$
7) $1^1/_5$ 8) $1^1/_3$
9) $^1/_2$ 10) $1^1/_4$

Exercise 4: 24
1) $2^1/_2$ 2) 2
3) $^1/_2$ 4) $^3/_8$
5) $2^4/_5$ 6) $2^1/_2$
7) $6^7/_8$ 8) $3^3/_4$

9) $2^1/_4$ 10) $1^1/_3$

Exercise 4: 25
1) $1^3/_7$ 2) $1^2/_7$
3) $1^1/_8$ 4) $^5/_{12}$
5) $^1/_2$ 6) $^5/_6$
7) $^1/_{16}$ 8) $^2/_{15}$
9) $^9/_{10}$ 10) $^3/_{10}$

Exercise 4: 26a
1) $1^2/_5$ 2) $^5/_{42}$
3) $2^2/_5$ 4) 3
5) $^3/_8$

Exercise 4: 26b
6) $2^{11}/_{14}$ 7) $2^3/_4$
8) $^{11}/_{14}$ 9) 0
10) $1^1/_2$

Exercise 4: 27a
1) 258 2) 195
3) 432 4) 248
5) 200

Exercise 4: 27b
6) 150 7) 490
8) 1,000 9) 182
10) 600

Exercise 4: 28
1) $^1/_2$ 2) $^1/_8$
3) $3^9/_{25}$ 4) $4^{27}/_{40}$
5) $^7/_{10}$ 6) $8^3/_{20}$
7) $6^4/_5$ 8) $3^1/_5$
9) $5^3/_4$ 10) $4^5/_8$

Exercise 4: 29
1) 0.625 2) 0.667
3) 3.167 4) 3.400
5) 4.143 6) 0.125
7) 3.444 8) 2.875
9) 0.571 10) 2.800

Exercise 4: 30a
1) $^5/_6$ 2) $^3/_4$
3) $^6/_7$

4) $^3/_4$ $^{13}/_{16}$ $^7/_8$
5) $^1/_5$ $^3/_{10}$ $^9/_{20}$ $^5/_8$

Exercise 4: 30b
6) $^3/_4$ 7) $^4/_7$
8) $^3/_5$ 9) $^3/_4$ $^9/_{16}$ $^3/_8$
10) $^5/_6$ $^2/_3$ $^3/_5$ $^1/_2$

Exercise 4: 31
1) 0.15 2) $^3/_8$
3) $^9/_{20}$ 4) $^7/_8$
5) 0.76 6) $^3/_5$
7) $^5/_8$ 8) 0.78
9) 0.59 $^5/_8$ 0.95
10) 0.13 $^1/_9$ $^1/_{12}$

Exercise 4: 32
1) $^1/_5$ 2) $^5/_{12}$
3) $^1/_2$ 4) $^2/_3$
5) 6yrs 6) $8^{13}/_{60}$
7) 14 8) 1
9) $1^7/_{15}$ 10) $4^{17}/_{42}$

Exercise 4: 33a
1) 49 children
2) 18 children
3) 45 pages
4) 16 chocolates
5) 154 trees
6) 55 children
7) 12 children

Exercise 4: 33b
8) 90
9) 48 mints
10) 30 stickers

Exercise 4: 34
1) $^1/_4$ 2) $^7/_{20}$
3) $^9/_{20}$ 4) 0.2
5) 0.4 6) $^2/_5$
7) $^{18}/_{25}$ 8) 1
9) 0.48 10) 1.08

Answers

11+ Maths
Year 5-7 Workbook 2

Exercise 4: 35
1) $1^5/_8$ or 1.625
2) $^1/_3$ 3) $7^{31}/_{42}$
4) $10^3/_{16}$ 5) $^6/_7$
6) 30 7) 110
8) a) $^5/_8$ b) $^1/_5$ c) $^3/_8$
9) a) $1^{11}/_{25}$ b) $2^2/_5$
   c) $3^1/_8$
10) a) $^{62}/_9$ b) $^{27}/_7$ c) $^{29}/_{10}$

Chapter Five
Money and Costs
Exercise 5: 1
1) 630p 2) 41p
3) 895p 4) 569p
5) 902p 6) £0.76
7) £15.40 8) £1.53
9) £0.07 10) £0.18

Exercise 5: 2
1) £11.69 2) £6.87
3) £11.24 4) £2.11
5) £356.44
6) £408.80 7) £5.50
8) £0.41
9) £600.57 10) £9.85

Exercise 5: 3
1) £15.89 2) £7.99
3) 6 weeks 4) £2.38
5) £159.96 6) 16p
7) £790 8) £12.25
9) £8,505 10) £30

Exercise 5: 4
1) £4.80 2) 15kg
3) £2.10; 2.5p
4) £2.70 5) £1.44
6) 65 glasses
7) £1.43 8) £10.50
9) £1,125 10) £9.60

Exercise 5: 5
1) 80 rupees
2) 36,000 rupees
3) £12.50 4) £2.80
5) £6.40 6) £20
7) £75 8) £200
9) 37.5 euros 10) £133.33

Exercise 5: 6
1) £34.40; £2.60
2) £10; £1.20
3) £31.30; £2.80
4) £12.80; £6.40
5) 11,000; £21.50
6) 3,500; £48
7) £88.50 8) £13
9) £145 10) £75.50

Exercise 5: 7
1) 11p 2) 16p
3) 10.77p 4) 12.5p
5) 13.33p 6) 1st - c
7) 2nd - a 8) 3rd - d
9) 4th - e 10) 5th - b

Exercise 5: 8
1) £9.00 2) 500g
3) 7 cans 4) £47.25
5) 190 yen 6) £3.50
7) 1,425 yen 8) 17p
9) £16.07 10) £70.80

Chapter Six
Measurement
Exercise 6: 1
1) 1kg 2) 10mm
3) 10mℓ 4) 1000mm
5) 1000kg 6) 1ℓ
7) 100cℓ 8) 10cℓ
9) 100cm 10) 1000m

Exercise 6: 2
1) 75mm or 7cm 5mm
2) 8,200g or 8kg 200g
3) 910cm or 9m 10cm
4) 368cℓ or 3,680mℓ
5) 6.43ℓ or 6ℓ 43cℓ
6) 1.73km or 1km 730m
7) 1.243kg or 1kg 243g
8) 0.037kg
9) 435cm and 2mm
10) 635cℓ or 6.35ℓ

Exercise 6: 3
1) 16.23km 2) 6.33ℓ
3) 77cm 4) 24.5kg
5) 3.21kg 6) 6.9t
7) 1.74ℓ 8) 2.76ℓ
9) 2.4m 10) 333 glasses

Exercise 6: 4
1) 3+ yards 2) 5kg
3) 10 pints 4) 3km
5) 6+ pounds 6) 10cm
7) 15 miles 8) 3 litres
9) 2 inches 10) 150cm

Exercise 6: 5
1) 51 yards 2) 50kg
3) 10,000 gallons 4) 66km
5) 8lbs or 7+lbs 6) 650kg
7) No 8) 6m
9) 1.5m 10) 23cm

Exercise 6: 6
1) 800mℓ 2) 4ℓ
3) 1.5kg 4) 25kg
5) 14ft 6) 5kg
7) No 8) 1kg
9) Bucket 10) 24m

Exercise 6: 7
1) 40cℓ 2) 250mℓ
3) 0.35ℓ 4) 0.25ℓ
5) 650mℓ 6) 0.1ℓ
7) 75cℓ
8) a) 160g b) 4.32kg
9) 0.023m 10) 147.3cm

11+ Maths
Year 5-7 Workbook 2

Answers

Exercise 6: 8
1) 8°C   2) -9°C
3) 9°C   4) -10°C
5) 4°C   6) 6°C
7) -1°C   8) 0°C
9) 1°C   10) -3°C

Exercise 6: 9
1) -24°C 2) 30°C
3) -27°C 4) 17°C
5) 3°C   6) 23°C
7) -1°C   8) 20°C
9) -1°C   10) 2°C

Exercise 6: 10
1) a) 210g b) 360g c) 300g
2) 1.5m   3) £17.00
4) a) £7.80   b) £10.80
   c) £4.20
5) £625   6) £5.12
7) a) 9.25m   b) 0.035m
8) a) 11.3m   b) 2.35m
   c) 4.6m
9) 510g, 0.501kg, 550g
10) a) 8t 700kg
    b) 5t 800kg

Chapter Seven
Averages
Exercise 7: 1
1) Mode   = 12
2) Median = 12
3) Range = 11
4) Mode   = 3
5) Median = 8.5
6) Range = 24
7) Mode   = 27
8) Median = 27.5
9) Median = 10
10) Range = 40

Exercise 7: 2a
1) 18   2) 3   3) 12
4) £1.00 5) 24.7°C

Exercise 7: 2b
6) £5.00   7) 7.25m

Exercise 7: 2c
8) 17 children 9) £7.45
10) 16 years

Exercise 7: 3
1) 27   2) 21
3) 21   4) 44
5) £17.50 6) £4.00
7) 4 cups 8) 6 cups
9) 6   10) 3 cups

Chapter Eight
Bases
Exercise 8: 1
1) 1010_2 2) 10001_2
3) 111_2 4) 1100_2
5) 11111_2 6) 15_{10}
7) 5_{10} 8) 6_{10}
9) 11_{10} 10) 29_{10}

Exercise 8: 2
1) 10010_2 2) 1110_2
3) 1000_2 4) 1110_2
5) 10000_2 6) 10011_2
7) 1010_2 8) 1001_2
9) 11000_2 10) 1011_2

Exercise 8: 3
1) 10020_3 2) 2011_3
3) 23_{10} 4) 66_{10}
5) 150_{10} 6) 304_5
7) 2034_5 8) 71_{10}
9) 104_{10} 10) 68_{10}

Exercise 8: 4
1) 10121_3 2) 122_3
3) 4343_5 4) 1043_5
5) 10102_3 6) 1100_3
7) 3440_5 8) 1314_5
9) Base 4 10) Base 2

Exercise 8: 5a
1) 2203_5 2) 1221_3
3) 4343_8 4) 2454_6
5) 563_9

Exercise 8: 5b
6) 11110_2 7) 23310_4
8) 4651_7 9) 22013_5
10) 7122_8

Exercise 8: 6
1) 220_3 2) 142_6
3) 1201_3 4) 423_8
5) 443_5 6) 1211_4
7) 344_{10} 8) 1223_7
9) 847_9 10) 1221_4

Exercise 8: 7
1) 116_7 2) 200_{10}
3) 1331_4 4) 5202_6
5) 3541_7 6) 637_8
7) a) 2401_5 b) 330_4
8) 32644_7 9) 1212_3
10) 2788_9

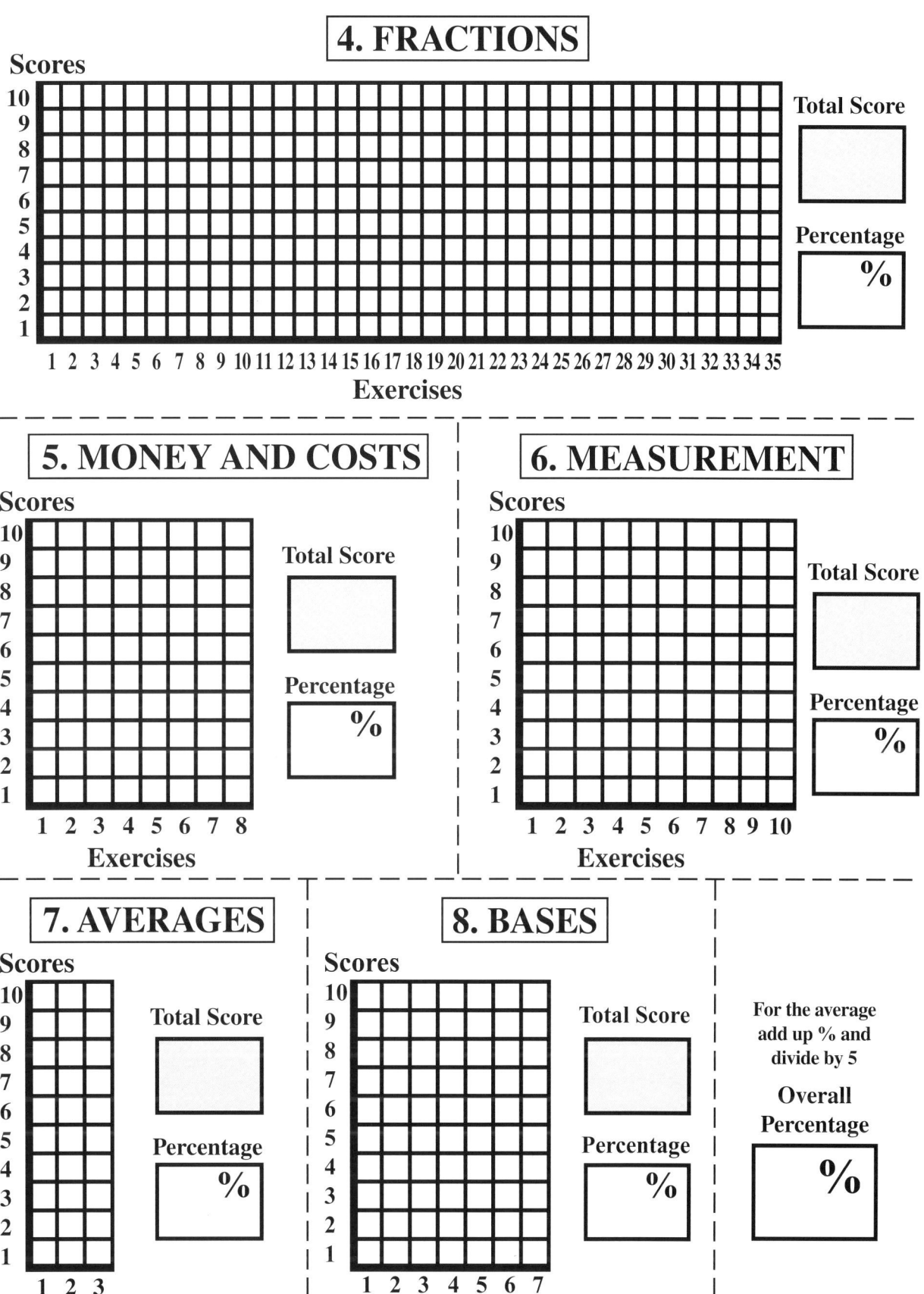

CERTIFICATE OF ACHIEVEMENT

This certifies

_____

has successfully completed

11+ Maths
Year 5–7
WORKBOOK 2

Overall percentage score achieved [ ] %

Comment _____

_____

Signed _____
(teacher/parent/guardian)

Date _____